Pilgrimage
of Hope

Pilgrimage of Hope

A COMMEMORATION OF TWENTY-THREE YEARS OF
DIAKONIA'S GOOD FRIDAY SERVICES

DIAKONIA COUNCIL OF CHURCHES
2009

Diakonia Council of Churches acknowledges with thanks the generous contributions towards the costs of publishing this book by:

 The KZN Provincial Government Office of the Premier

and

Norwegian Church Aid

Published by **DIAKONIA COUNCIL OF CHURCHES**
Diakonia Centre, 20 Diakonia Avenue, Durban 4001
PO Box 61341, Bishopsgate 4008
Phone: 031 310-3500
Fax: 031 310-3502
E-mail: the.director@diakonia.org.za
Website: www.diakonia.org.za

Photographs and press clippings from the Independent Newspapers are gratefully acknowledged.

Writing, collation and editing by Sue Brittion

Design and production by Graphicos

ISBN 1-874985-99-5

Pilgrimage of Hope
A Commemoration of twenty-three years of
Diakonia's Good Friday Services

Foreword: Our Pilgrimage of Hope

A concerned Christian wrote this verse:

When Jesus came to Golgotha
they hanged him on a tree,
they drove great nails through hands and feet
and made their Calvary.
They crowned him with a crown of thorns
red were his wounds and deep
for those were crude and cruel days
and human flesh was cheap.

When Jesus came to Durban
they simply passed him by
they never hurt a hair of him
they only let him die.
For they had grown more tender
they would not cause him pain
they only passed him in the street
and left him in the rain.

Still Jesus cried 'Forgive them
for they know not what they do'
and still it rained a summer rain
that drenched him through and through
The crowds went home and left the street
without a soul to see,
and Jesus crouched against the wall
and cried for Calvary.

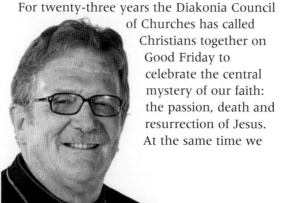

For twenty-three years the Diakonia Council of Churches has called Christians together on Good Friday to celebrate the central mystery of our faith: the passion, death and resurrection of Jesus. At the same time we have tried to conscientise and make people aware of Jesus suffering among us today.

In the first years of the Good Friday service we were in solidarity with, and prayed for, all who were cruelly oppressed by the apartheid regime: those who were killed, those who were displaced, those in prison, detention, those on Robben Island. We prayed each year for the end of that vicious, unjust system. Our prayers were answered. Since then we have been in solidarity with those who suffer economic injustice, abused women and children, those infected and affected by HIV/AIDS, the unemployed, those living in abject poverty.

We keep alive in the hearts of our brothers and sisters the unconditional love of Jesus on that first Good Friday and of Jesus calling us to minister to him in the poor and the most abandoned of our day.
"Whatever you do to the least of my brothers and sisters you do to me."

May this commemorative book be an inspiration to us all on our own pilgrimage of hope.

Bishop Barry Wood OMI
Chairperson: Diakonia Council of Churches

Dedication

This book is dedicated to Paddy Kearney.

As the pioneer and leader of the organisation founded by the late Archbishop Denis Hurley to serve church and community, Paddy has epitomised the quality of diakonia – the Greek word meaning 'service to the people.'

Diakonia was set up to be a stimulus and resource for the churches' work for a free and just society, as well as a tool to motivate and help the churches play this role. Paddy has helped others to grow in their ability to serve the churches in the struggle for justice and human rights for all.   He has always been modest and self-effacing, sharing the praise due for his many achievements with the team of Diakonia staff and representatives of member churches.

Paddy has helped others discover that true service/diakonia needs to start where people are. In the case of the churches, the common thread through all the work of all churches, no matter how different they may appear, is worship.

And so, early in its life as an organisation, Diakonia started offering worship and liturgy to its member churches, with a special focus on the injustices of the world that cry out to God for mercy, compassion and justice, as well as for action on the part of Christians.

When the Good Friday services began, many church people recognised them as a way of coming together in prayer and praise, in the reading of the scriptures and proclamation of the gospel, in expression of their own great suffering, and the suffering of so many other people. It was a way of offering all this to God in solidarity with others, as a way of inviting God to strengthen the worshippers to continue the struggles of their lives and those of the communities around them.

The Good Friday services owe their inspiration, ethos and reputation to Paddy, and to his ability to inspire many others to work hard, creatively and with minute attention to detail in the planning and arranging of these services over so many years. Without Paddy this great tradition would not be such an integral and important part of the annual life of both the churches and the city of Durban.

We salute Paddy for what has so long been the key annual event of the organisation that he founded, and hope that this book captures its essence.

Durban, March 2009

ARCHBISHOP Denis Hurley leads worshippers to Durban Central Prison where 300 people yesterday sang hymns and prayed in solidarity with treason trialists and others who are in prison.

Daily News Reporter

D.N. 6/4/85

Hurley leads 300 in march through Durban to prison

MORE than 300 people marched through the city-centre to Durban's Central Prison yesterday as an act of solidarity with all people suffering in South Africa.

"We proceed in solidarity with the treason trialists who have fought to help change our society to one based on love, justice and peace," said Mr Paddy Kearney, director of Diakonia, a church organisation.

The crowd started their worship service in the Central Methodist Church in Aliwal Street and then were led into the streets by Archbishop Denis Hurley carrying a large wooden cross.

Durban's City Police had demarcated a section of the road that the procession would follow and had also sealed off the section of Commercial Road that runs alongside the prison.

The crowd marched along the road singing Easter hymns. In the shadow of the prison walls they continued the service of Bible readings, hymns, prayers and short addresses.

Archbishop Hurley, addressing the crowd, said this Good Friday had a deep significance as they stood outside the prison.

"We enter too into deep sympathy with those inside the walls and those in prison throughout South Africa, especially for their dedication to liberation, peace and love, and in a very particular way for our 16 friends facing treason charges who know about our presence outside these walls and are lifted up and encouraged by that presence," he said.

In a statement outlining the purpose of the procession, Diakonia, the organisers, said that Jesus went through a similar experience to the treason trialists.

"He paid the ultimate cost, death on the cross. His teachings and example rocked the Roman establishment and we are now called to follow the example of our Lord's ministry of service and liberation."

A YOUNG BOY WAS BEING HANGED before all the inmates of a Nazi extermination camp together with two adults – each of them guilty of some trivial infringement of the camp's rules. Whereas the two adults died immediately, the boy was so light that his death struggle lasted for over half an hour. As the hundreds of prisoners watched this excruciating spectacle and were even compelled to walk past the gallows so that they would learn the price of any disobedience, one man turned to another and asked: *"Where is God now?"* His neighbour heard a voice within him answer: *"Where is God? Here – hanging on the gallows."*

This shocking incident, recorded in Elie Wiesel's *Night,* reminds us of a profound truth: suffering is a revelation of God's presence. The gospel account of the last judgment tells us that we will all be judged on how we have responded to the suffering we see around us. *"For I was hungry and you gave me food, I was thirsty and you gave me drink, I was a stranger and you made me welcome, naked and you clothed me, sick and you visited me, in prison and you came to see me."* (Mt. 25:35,36)

In 1985, apartheid South Africa was in deep crisis. Repression had reached such intensity that Diakonia's ecumenical colleagues in the Western Cape were openly praying for the downfall of the regime. Their hope was that churches and ecumenical organisations throughout South Africa would take up the call. When this request was raised in the Diakonia Executive, despite admiration for this challenging example, there was little enthusiasm to do the same in Durban. The gravity of the national situation was recognised, but Diakonia wanted to respond in its own way.

As Diakonia considered various options, the Executive remembered that 16 United Democratic Front (UDF) leaders were in Durban's Central Prison awaiting trial on charges of treason. They were known to Diakonia and some of them had worked closely with Diakonia in campaigns for a more just society: Paul David, Mewa Ramgobin, Sam Kikine and, above all, Archie Gumede. Archie was not only one of the UDF presidents but a deacon of the United Congregational Church which he represented on the Diakonia Council. The Executive knew that these 16 people were not treasonous but true patriots. The only difference between them and members of the Diakonia Executive was that they were more courageous in expressing their opposition to apartheid.

The church's ancient tradition was also remembered, and the decision was taken that on Good Friday a cross would be carried through Durban's streets to the Central Prison to show solidarity with the treason trialists and many others who were unjustly imprisoned. Diakonia's lawyer, Chris Albertyn, advised that the service should not go ahead without official permission, because the procession would be broken up before it even started. He helped Diakonia draft an official application to Durban's Chief Magistrate and Chief Constable.

This application indicated that the procession would take place at dawn on Good Friday – that time was chosen because it would not interfere with any other Good Friday services – from Central Methodist Church to the Central Prison. It would be in total silence and there would be no placards or banners, but church leaders would carry a large wooden cross. No speeches would be made outside the prison but prayers would be said and Good Friday hymns would be sung. Most surprisingly, permission was granted. The authorities must have felt that it would not look good to ban the carrying of a cross on Good Friday.

And so it was that people gathered at 6.00am in Central Methodist Church, a group of about 300 people from many different churches and from all over Durban. Bishop Michael Nuttall of the Anglican Church led a meditation on the meaning of the cross, and Diakonia Chairperson, the Revd Wesley Mabuza of the Methodist Church, reminded the congregation that, in carrying the cross to the Central Prison, they would be highlighting all the sufferings of people in South Africa. Prison, he said, had become the symbol of apartheid repression.

As the procession set off along what was then known as Aliwal Street, leaders of Diakonia's eight member churches took turns carrying a two-metre-high cross. Following them were guests of honour, wives and children of the treason trialists, in particular Edith Gumede, Ela Ramgobin (Gandhi) and Ursula David, followed by the rest of the congregation.

It was puzzling to see white men in overalls apparently doing road work along the route at this early hour on a public holiday. It turned out that they were security police carefully monitoring the solemn procession, perhaps fearing that it might suddenly turn into a raucous mob chanting freedom songs and waving banners and placards that had been carefully concealed under the robes of priests and ministers.

Something else was extraordinary. When the procession reached the Central Prison and stood opposite the entrance, voices were heard from inside joining in the singing of Good Friday hymns. Roman Catholic Archbishop Denis Hurley, who led the prayers outside the prison and who had visited the treason trialists earlier in the week, said that he had informed them about the service and they were *"strengthened, uplifted and encouraged by our prayers and support."*

When the service ended with the anthem *"Nkosi sikelel' iAfrika"* (God bless Africa), suddenly the doors of the prison opened and out came a large number of security police who had taken up positions there, presumably to deal with any sudden "storming of the Bastille" to free the 16 treason trialists.

Little did those who took part in this unique service on 5 April 1985 know that they were starting an annual tradition which continues 24 years later and will in all probability continue for as long as there is a Diakonia. The Good Friday service and the carrying of the cross through Durban's streets has become the central event in the local ecumenical calendar – a unique "annual general meeting" of all Diakonia's member churches when about 4 000 people gather to reflect on some aspect of contemporary suffering in the light of Jesus' passion and death.

As you will see in the photographs, graphics, extracts from the liturgies and the accounts of the Good Friday services in this book, this consistent theme has been presented in creative ways about a variety of issues. The annual Good Friday service is an icon of all Diakonia's work to help the churches play a leading role in the transformation of society.

"I shall be in agony until the end of time" God says.
"I shall be crucified until the end of time."

Prayers of Life by Michel Quoist

Good Friday Procession

Before this Good Friday ends I want to write down my congratulations to Diakonia for the service and procession of this morning. I was very deeply impressed by the prayerfulness, the good order and the sincerity which was so evident throughout. Clearly a lot of very careful planning and work had gone into it – and for that I say "Thank-you."

Everything – the readings and meditations, the singing and the procession – were such that people could not fail to enter into the spirit of it all and give full participation.

I hope and pray that those in the Central Prison were able to hear something of it all, and be consoled and strengthened in the knowledge that they were not forgotten or alone.

This experience gave to my Good Friday this year a new and very significant dimension, bringing the suffering of Christ more vividly into the present moment than I have ever known it before.

May God continue to bless the fine work you are doing.

Yours sincerely in Christ,
Sr Nancy Needham f.m.m.
Seaview

Prayer and solidarity with our leaders

I learned the significance of Good Friday in early childhood when we learned the teachings of all the scriptures of the main religions. Significant too was the fact that my grandfather was assassinated on a Friday. So Fridays became a day of special prayer for us. It is a day when we fast and a day when we contemplate how we can make a difference in the world.

So, when many of our leaders, and in particular Baba Archie Gumede, were held in the Central Prison, we requested Archbishop Hurley to have a service outside the prison. He agreed, and so the first march in 1985 was to the space opposite the Central Prison, where the ICC now stands. We sang hymns and the service culminated with *Nkosi sikelel' iAfrika*, hoping that the crescendo would be heard in the prison – and it was. It was a moving service and Archbishop Hurley spoke of the meaning and significance of sacrifice. He blessed those who were being held in prisons and those who had given their lives and those being repressed under the many oppressive laws.

Since then, the Good Friday services held a further significance for us in the struggle against apartheid. Baba Archie Gumede and other leaders of the movement were regular participants in the services. It became a day when we prayed for strength and guidance to be able to continue in our struggle against the oppression and suffering of our people.

Now we have found a new significance in the Good Friday marches, when we rededicate ourselves to the cause of the millions of deprived people and the suffering of so many due to the HIV pandemic, poverty and inequality. I have tried to participate in every march, although due to unforeseen circumstances I have had to miss some. But the significance of the day is never forgotten.

Ela Gandhi

A memory of the first Diakonia Good Friday service

Many years ago, my father attended the Methodist Synod in Pretoria. It was the first time he, as a representative, was faced with the challenge of shaking hands with a black man. This simple greeting changed his life.

I had a similar exposure at the first Diakonia Good Friday service ever held in Durban. It was decided to process from the Central Methodist Church to the old Prison, situated where the new extension to the International Convention Centre has been erected. A number of political prisoners, many of whom were known to members of Diakonia, were being held in the prison at the time. We stood on the old railway line and, as a token of solidarity, sang songs and hymns together concluding our service of worship 'with' those inside. This exposure was an unforgettable experience for me and changed my life.

Exposure visits, with the object of increasing the sensitivity of people to one another in our polarised community, became a very important feature of my ministry from then on.

Revd Dr Norman Hudson
Previous Chairperson of Diakonia

Solidarity with all those in prison

We want to be with Jesus where he is suffering today.

We want to pray for all who suffer, and in a special way for all those in prison, particularly those on Robben Island, in Pollsmoor, and especially the sixteen treason trialists being held here.

We enter into deep sympathy with those inside these walls and those in prison throughout South Africa, especially for their dedication to liberation, peace and love, and in a very particular way for our sixteen friends facing treason charges, who know about our presence outside these walls and are uplifted, strengthened and encouraged by our prayers and support.

We pray that South Africans may all be free from the prison of apartheid.

Nkosi sikelel' iAfrika

Nkosi sikelel' iAfrika	God bless Africa
Maluphakanyis' uphondo lwayo	Let your name be praised
Yiva nemithandazo yethu	Listen to our prayers
Nkosi sikelela	Lord, bless us
Thina lusapho lwayo	Your people
Woza Moya	Come, Holy Spirit
Sikelela Nkosi sikelela	Bless, Lord, bless
Woza Moya	Come, Holy Spirit
Sikelela Nkosi sikelela	Bless, Lord, bless
Woza Moya oyingcwele	Come, Holy Spirit
Nkosi sikelela	Lord, bless us
Thina lusapho lwayo	Your people
Morena Boloka sechaba sa Hesu	Lord, save your people
O fedisa dintwa la matshwenyeho	End wars and suffering
Osiboloke	Save
Osiboloke	Save
Osiboloke Morena	Save, Lord,
Osiboloke	Save
Sechaba sa Hesu	Your people
Sechaba sa Afrika	The people of Africa

At the head of the procession, the Reverend Mcebisi Xundu carries a cross, assisted by the Very Reverend George Purves.

Peace service held at prison after march

by Carmel Rickard

SINGING voices from inside the Durban Central Prison joined with the 300 people who held a dawn Good Friday service outside the walls of the jail.

The service followed a procession led by prominent church leaders including Catholic Archbishop Denis Hurley and Anglican Bishop Michael Nuttall. They carried a two-metre wooden cross through the streets of Durban to the prison where 16 UDF and trade union leaders are awaiting trial for treason.

Guests of honour in the procession and at the service were the wives and children of some of the 16, including Mrs Edith Gumede, wife of UDF president Mr Archie Gumede, himself a deacon in the Congregational Church.

The solemn procession is a ritual practiced by the Christian Church for many centuries — that of visiting prisoners on Good Friday.

Mr Paddy Kearney, director of Diakonia, the church agency which organised the procession and service, said the procession was called "to pray for peace, justice and reconciliation and for an end to apartheid which imprisons everyone in South Africa."

Prayers were said for all in prison in South Africa, particularly those on Robben Island, in Pollsmoor (where Nelson Mandela is imprisoned) and for the 16 treason-trialists in the Durban jail.

Archbishop Denis Hurley leads the service outside the Stanger Street prison.

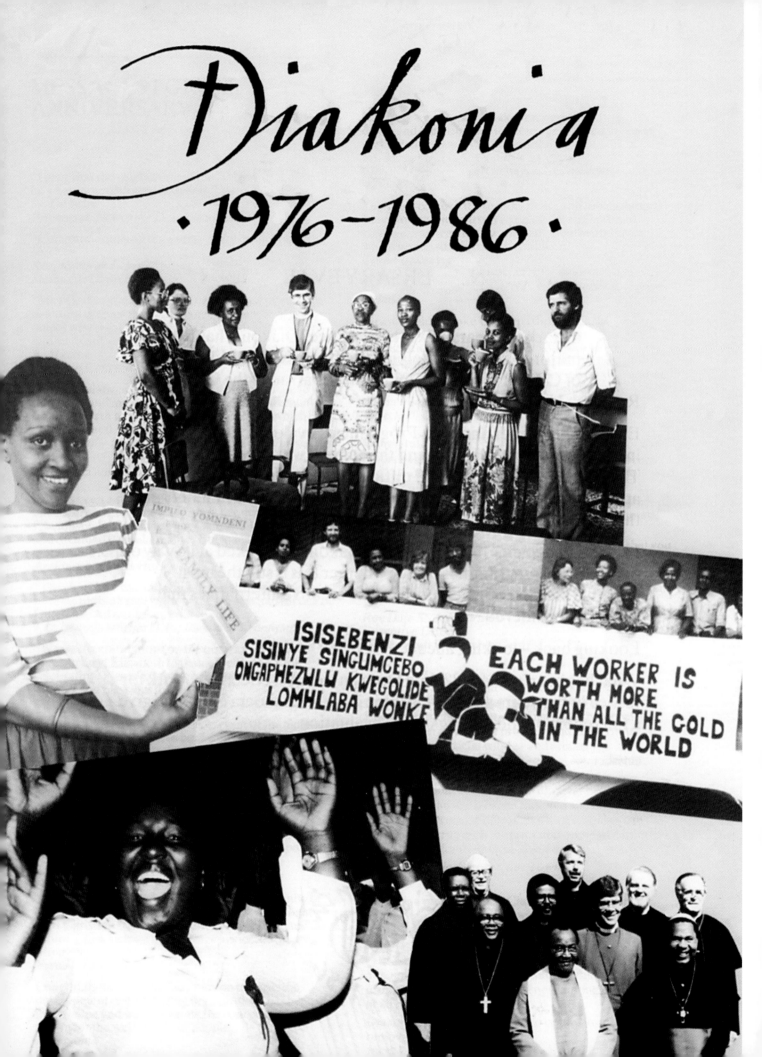

Diakonia
· 1976 - 1986 ·

ISISEBENZI
SISINYE SINGUMCEBO
ONGAPHEZULU KWEGOLIDE
LOMHLABA WONKE

EACH WORKER IS
WORTH MORE
THAN ALL THE GOLD
IN THE WORLD

THE CRISIS DEEPENS

The year of the first Good Friday service, 1985, was a time of greatly intensified crisis in South Africa. The deepening political crisis, a deteriorating economy, the growth of militance and resistance and increasing state repression, especially through the use of the South African Defence Force (SADF) in the townships and the declaration of a State of Emergency, created new demands for all involved in working for justice.

Durban exploded after the assassination of civil rights lawyer Victoria Mxenge on 1 August 1985. Within days more than 100 people were killed and 1000 injured in a crisis that started at Inanda-Phoenix but spread to many townships.

A second major crisis took place in January 1986, when more than 120 were killed and 15 000 lost their homes in 'faction fights' at No. 5 Umbongintwini. Between these two crises, many homes of political activists were burned down in the townships, and many other activists fled for safety – fearing attacks by vigilante groups and *'amabutho'* (warriors).

Diakonia was very involved in assisting the victims of these crises, as well as probing more deeply to find the causes and urge its member churches to address themselves to those causes. These tasks challenged the organisation to the limits of its staffing and other resources. Ironically, it was at times like these, when Diakonia was attempting to serve people as generously as possible, that state harrassment was often at its most intense too – resulting in the detentions of two staff members in the midst of the August 1985 crisis.

The local and national crisis left Diakonia with many questions about its future role. These questions were timely, because the organisation had already decided that the most important aspect of the10th Anniversary of its founding in 1976 would be a major evaluation.

No Good Friday service was planned for 1986. At the time it was not seen as an annual event. The focus of the year was on marking the ten years of Diakonia's work in the middle of the intensifying crisis.

10TH ANNIVERSARY, EVALUATION AND CELEBRATIONS

Diakonia's evaluation was to assess its role over the previous ten years and look forward to see how it would need to change to meet new challenges. Especially Diakonia tried to determine how it could help member churches to prepare for the very different South Africa that lay ahead – and to play its full role in shaping that future.

The organisation was assisted in an intense, participatory process of evaluation during April and May 1986 by Mildred Neville, former General Secretary of the Catholic Institute for International Relations in London, and Vish Suparsad, Director of the Durban-based Community Research Unit.

Several celebratory events were held to mark the 10th anniversary. A tea party was held for tenants of the Ecumenical Centre (as it was then named) on 3 February, to mark the date in 1976 on which the Diakonia offices opened for the first time. On 25 March a Liberation Supper marked the date on which Diakonia's inaugural meeting was held in 1976. And on 10 May a 'Diakonia Day' saw parish social action groups and other justice & peace groups sharing their activities, a special children's programme, and a final moving and creative time of worship as the culmination of the celebrations.

The basis of Diakonia's work is that it has made an option for the poor, in the sense that it is on the side of the poor.

Diakonia is an organisation which tries to listen to what the poor and marginalised are saying and, in some senses, to be present with them in their experiences and their suffering.

From Evaluation Report 1986

The aim of Diakonia is, in obedience to God's command, to support the principal forces bringing about justice and liberation in South Africa, and to involve the member churches as fully as possible in this support.

Statement of aims adopted by Diakonia's Council 1986

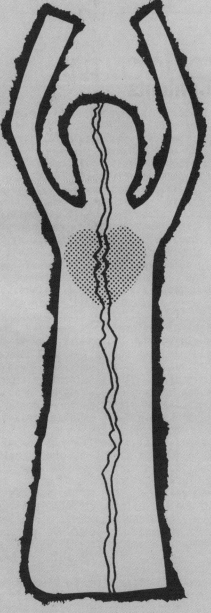

diakonia
10
1976 - 1986

Yahweh
has
Sent me
to bring
Good news
to the
Poor,
to bind up
hearts
that are
Broken,
to Proclaim
Liberty
to
Captives

Isaiah :61

Diakonia Annual Report 1986

Diakonia
· 1976–1986 ·

WHERE THE SPIRIT OF THE LORD IS

THERE IS FREEDOM

Liberation Supper

The Liberation Supper held on 25 March 1986, the 10th anniversary of Diakonia's inaugural meeting, was a Passover Meal with a difference.

Its focus was not only on the liberation of the Israelites from Egypt but on the current struggle for liberation in South Africa. Thus, the biblical account of the sufferings inflicted on the ancient Israelites by their Egyptian oppressors was contextualised when speakers described the sufferings endured by South Africans in 1986.

The traditional passover foods were eaten to the accompaniment of ritual questions and answers in a family setting – a group of children asking the questions in turn, and the roles of mother and father of the family being taken by Mary Mkhwanazi of the South African Domestic Workers' Association (SADWA) and Archbishop Denis Hurley, Diakonia's Chairperson at the time. The traditional meal of roast lamb was served, and people sang relevant hymns and songs at various points during the ceremony.

As the closing words of the ceremony reminded people, much needed to be done before the liberation that Christ promised could become a reality in South Africa. With this in mind, people were invited to join hands and pledge themselves to work for justice.

service for children in detention

 GOOD FRIDAY
6.30 am · April 17th

CENTRAL METHODIST CHURCH
Aliwal Street

STATE OF EMERGENCY

In 1986, Diakonia celebrated its 10th anniversary and completed an in-depth evaluation of all its work over those ten years, just in time to face the biggest challenge of the ten years – the State of Emergency imposed on 12 June.

The State of Emergency began dramatically for Diakonia and the other organisations working in the Ecumenical Centre (now the Diakonia Centre), which was surrounded by Security Police and casspirs (armoured vehicles) from the early hours of the morning of 12 June.

Only after an urgent application had been brought in the Supreme Court and after further negotiations between their lawyers and those representing the police were staff admitted to their offices late in the afternoon, and then the offices were systematically searched.

Much of Diakonia's work was concerned with communicating information and making the truth known. This was made extremely difficult because of the State of Emergency.

Diakonia's work also depended very much on contact with community organisations and attending meetings for the purpose of coordination. Both these activities became problematic as a result of the State of Emergency, which was successful in breaking down the established links between organisations. The vast number of detentions – an estimated forty thousand people, many of them under the age of eighteen – as well as of people in hiding, made communication between organisations very difficult. Towards the end of 1986 and in the first months of 1987, there was a disturbing number of mass murders in Natal townships such as Mphophomeni, KwaMakhutha and Mpumalanga, where members of the Congress of South African Trade Unions (Cosatu) and youth leaders linked to the UDF were assassinated, adding a further obstacle to democratic organisation in the townships. The future looked challenging and bleak indeed.

CHILDREN IN DETENTION

The Black Sash initiated a national and international *'Free the Children Campaign'* to actively work for the release of the many children held in detention under the State of Emergency. Diakonia jointly organised a Good Friday *'Service for Children in Detention'* together with the campaign organisers in Durban, and on 18 March sent out a letter inviting all church ministers in the Greater Durban area to participate.

Diakonia distributed thousands of copies of a leaflet reminding Christians that Jesus was also arrested, and explaining the injustice and sufferings of detention.

On 10 April, a week before the service was due to be held, the Commissioner of the South African Police issued a Notice under the Public Safety Act making it an offence to participate *"in any campaign, project or action aimed at accomplishing the release of persons .. detained under section 22 or 29 of the Internal Security Act 1982 .. or regulation 3 of the Security Regulations."*

After consultation with its Executive and with its lawyers, a media release was issued, stating that the Good Friday dawn service, jointly called by the "Free The Children Campaign" and Diakonia had been cancelled and that, following legal advice, Diakonia – an organisation of 8 Christian denominations – would hold an ecumenical prayer service on Good Friday starting at 6.30am. It continued: *"This Good Friday service, in keeping with the ancient Christian tradition of praying for prisoners on Good Friday, is being called to pray for all in detention – especially children."* Over 600 people gathered at Central Methodist Church on 17 April for a service focussing on Jesus' passion and death. Bishop Philip Russell, former Anglican Archbishop of Cape Town, preached a moving sermon.

The congregation then walked through the streets of Durban's city centre to St Paul's Anglican Church. Sixty members of the clergy carried crosses one metre high, as a way of recalling the suffering of the sixty children being held in detention at that time in Durban's Westville Prison. A three metre cross symbolising all other detainees was carried at the front of the procession.

At the end of the service in St Paul's, relatives of detainees were invited to take home one of the symbolic crosses. Clergy and nuns were also encouraged to take a cross with them, to use in their own Good Friday liturgies, along with the special *Prayer for Children in Detention* which had been distributed nationally and internationally for use on Good Friday.

This service, like the one two years earlier at the Central Prison, ended with the hymn *"All hail the power of Jesus' name"* – a reminder that the cross is not the last word – but rather the victory and triumph of the resurrection. A reminder also that Jesus' death and resurrection gives people the power to triumph over detentions and all the injustices of apartheid.

God sees and weeps

Extract of sermon by Archbishop Philip Russell

It does not matter whether there are a thousand detained children or just one. One child who is detained without trial, who may or may not be tortured, is part of the reason God sent his Son into the world to die on the cross.

I can never understand detention without trial. I can never understand those who torture prisoners, and only vicariously can I understand what it must mean to be the relative of someone who is detained and perhaps tortured.

Although I find it difficult to understand, I believe God can understand – God sees and weeps.

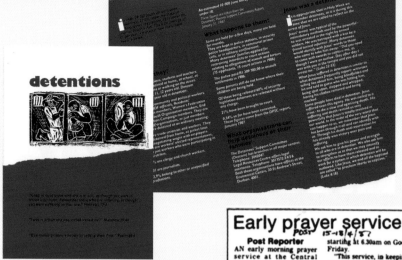

detentions

Early prayer service

POST 15–18/4/87

Post Reporter

AN early morning prayer service at the Central Methodist Church, Aliwal Street, will replace the Good Friday church service which had been cancelled following the emergency regulations regarding detainees.

A statement by Diakonia, an organisation of eight Christian denominations, said that dawn service, jointly called by the Free the Children Campaign and Diakonia, had been cancelled and that Diakonia, following legal advice, would hold an ecumenical prayer service at the Central Methodist Church.

starting at 6.30am on Good Friday.

"This service, in keeping with the ancient Christian tradition of praying for prisoners on Good Friday, is being called to pray for all in detention — especially children.

"The service — scheduled to last until 8am — will be led by the Most Rev Denis Hurley, Catholic Archbishop of Durban; the Rt Rev Michael Nuttall, Anglican Bishop of Natal; and other Christian leaders. The sermon will be preached by the Rt Rev Bishop Philip Russell, former Archbishop of Cape Town."

Masses join clergy in

Special service for detainees

Mercury Reporter

HUNDREDS of people joined parents of children in detention and more than 30 clergymen of all denominations bearing symbolic crosses in a march from Durban's Central Methodist Church to St Paul's Anglican Church opposite the main post office yesterday.

The procession took place after a special day-break Good Friday service for child detainees, led by the Rev Philip Russel, the former Anglican Archbishop of Cape Town, Archbishop Denis Hurley and Bishop Michael Nuttall.

Restrictions

The clergymen, carrying a large wooden cross and 60 smaller ones, led the multiracial congregation of more than 300 people along a kilometre-long procession across the city centre.

Although restrictions imposed by police last weekend prohibit public appeals for the release of detainees at any political meeting, the public display of an ornament with a political message were not affected.

Clergyman bearing symbolic crosses lead hundreds in a march from

THE TIMES FRIDAY JUNE 13 1986

Ottawa gets tough ● Europe wants action ● V

South African troops and security police patrolling outside the Ecumenical Centre in Durban yesterday to prevent anyone from entering while a search warrant was being issued in the nationwide clampdown on activism.

Top black leaders held in security crackdown

From Ray Kennedy
Johannesburg

Among the hundreds of anti-apartheid activists detained in South Africa yesterday was Mr Aubrey Mokoena, publicity secretary of the Release Mandela Campaign. A member of the national executive of the United Democratic Front, he has been detained

without trial several times since 1974.

He first came to political prominence at the University of the North – from which he was expelled over anti-apartheid protests – as a founder-member of the South African Students' Organization.

He became a leading figure

in the black consciousness movement in Soweto and was detained for seven months after the 1976 uprising. Six months after his release he was again detained without trial for 394 days.

A further period of detention without trial followed in 1984, during the UDF's campaign against the constitutional referendum and elections in

the Coloured and Indian houses of the tricameral Parliament.

Another prominent activist detained yesterday was detained president of the Azanian People's Organization, Mr Saths Cooper.

In 1976 he was jailed for six years after he organised pro-Frelimo rallies following Mozambique's independence.

GOOD Friday in Durban was a prayer day for the release of detainees. A procession of about 600 Christians took to the streets singing hymns which brought traffic in the city centre to a standstill. The group, led by prominent church leaders, marched through Aliwal Street, Pine Street and past the Central Methodist Church to St Paul's Anglican Church

SALON PARISIENNE TEL 321688

The KINGS RESTAURANT

Detai

LAST week's proclam of restrictions on cal the release of detai prevented publication prayer by the Black Sa an advertisement in the day Tribune. However Commissioner of Pe General Johan Coetzee this week that the n was not intended to prayers for the relea

Opening prayer

We attend this service out of obedience to God's command to *"keep in mind those who are in prison as though in prison with them, and those who are badly treated, since you are in the one body."* We gather to pray earnestly this Good Friday that God will hear the prayer of detainees, that God will protect them, especially the youngest and most vulnerable, that God will set them free.

Prayer for the children in detention

Lord Jesus
  you experienced in person
  the sufferings and the death of a prisoner of conscience.
You were plotted against,
  betrayed by a friend,
  and arrested under cover of darkness
  by men who came with clubs and swords.
You were tortured, beaten and humiliated,
  and sentenced to an agonising death
  though you had done no wrong.

Be now with prisoners of conscience throughout the world,
  and with all the detainees in our prisons.
Be especially today with the children in detention.
Be with them in the silence of solitary confinement,
  in the loneliness of separation from their families.
Be with them in their fear
  of what might happen to them.
Be with their parents who suffer,
  as your mother suffered at the foot of your cross.

Give us your power
  to break their chains and open the gates of freedom.
Work with us, Lord,
  that your kingdom of justice may be established now amongst us.

Closing prayer

We pray for all detainees who suffer in isolation this frightful restriction upon their freedom.   We believe Jesus is present in a special way in the detained children.

  We ask pardon if we have been too cold and indifferent about the fate of the detainees, the fate and suffering of the children.

Living our faith in love like Jesus

It is my honour and privilege to share how the annual ecumenical Good Friday services, organised by the Diakonia Council of Churches, have impacted my life over the past 22 years. This initiative was instituted at the time in the face of the worst political violence and injustices we were experiencing, particularly here in KwaZulu-Natal, under the draconian apartheid laws perpetrated by the then Nationalist regime.

At each service I felt personally challenged, through worship, music, dance, drama and relevant themes, by a profound spiritual awakening – a conscious awareness of God's overwhelming love for all humankind. Each experience redefined the meaning of the crucifixion of Christ, who, himself having no sin, broke the power of sin for our salvation. It is still difficult to fathom the indignity, the shame endured by Jesus – stripped naked, flogged, garlanded with thorns, spat upon and mocked. Nothing compares to the self-restraint revealed by Jesus on that first Good Friday. What a saviour!

I had the most humbling experience of being chosen as one of the cross-bearers for several years. Carrying the cross with my sisters and brothers in Christ, walking through the streets to St Paul's Church, and in later years to the steps of the Durban City Hall, in absolute inner stillness, listening to the chiming of the church bells and infinitely aware of my own unworthiness, made me realise how vital it is for us as Christians to live our faith in love like Jesus.

Again, the flowering of the cross, a symbolic act of our faith in our risen Christ, marked an occasion to restore dignity and self-worth through economic and educational empowerment with those suffering pain and poverty, for recommitment and re-dedication to a positive involvement.

Thank you, Diakonia, for the tremendous transformative role you play in awakening our conscience and broadening our vision to see Christ in others.

Enid Fourie

CRUCIFIXION, DEATH and RESURRECTION

DETENTIONS, BANNINGS ...FREEDOM

Ecumenical Service
GOOD FRIDAY · 1st APRIL 1988 · 6.30am
Preacher: Rev.Stanley Mogoba
President-Elect Methodist Church

Central Methodist Church
Aliwal Street · Durban

Issued by Diakonia, 20 St Andrews Street, Durban

1988

This image, taken at the 1988 Good Friday service, appears as a detail on the cover of a biography of Archbishop Denis Hurley, entitled "Guardian of the Light" being published by Continuum (New York & London). The author is Paddy Kearney who directed Diakonia from 1976 to 2004.

Source: KNA-Bild, Bonn

RESPONSE TO REPRESSION

State repression increased sharply during 1987, with emergency restrictions placed on nineteen organisations, including the UDF and Cosatu, as well as the *New Nation* newspaper and a number of individuals. These restrictions effectively prevented them from operating at all.

Because of the weak state of community and student organisations, Diakonia staff found that quite a lot of their time had to be devoted to assisting such organisations to begin functioning again despite all the limitations imposed by the State of Emergency.

In planning for 1988 it was found that this concentration on assistance to organisations had led to some neglect of the work of involving member churches, and so Diakonia decided that work with the churches should enjoy the highest priority during 1988. Many people looked to the church more than ever to ensure that the struggle for justice continued.

SILENCING OF ORGANISATIONS

The 1988 Good Friday service focussed on the awesome *'silencing of God'* on the first Good Friday and linked this with the silencing of organisations, individuals and the media. It was stressed that the silencing of the voices calling for justice in South Africa through the restrictions was, in fact, a silencing of God, because *"the desire for the truth, justice and freedom comes from God, and is a mark that we are made in God's image."*

During the service, once again held in the Central Methodist Church, nineteen people, representing the silenced organisations, took their place in the sanctuary facing the congregation and wearing gags, as the aims and work of organisations they represented was explained, as well as how closely this work related to the work of the church. The sermon was preached by the Revd Stanley Mogoba, President-Elect of the Methodist Church.

The nineteen gagged people, with church leaders, clergy, nuns and theological students, then led nearly a thousand people up the main street of Durban to St Paul's Anglican Church. They carried large crosses and processed in complete silence.

After a commitment shared by the whole congregation, church leaders symbolically removed the gags of the nineteen. This action reminded everyone that the silencing of Jesus on Good Friday gave way to the triumph of the resurrection, when his voice was *"freed to resound through all time and history."*

At the end of the service, the crosses and gags were distributed for use in other Good Friday services later that day.

A moving and unusual service took place a short while after the end of the ecumenical Good Friday service. It took place on Battery Beach No. 1, opposite the headquarters of Natal Command of the SADF. Black Sash members used four of the crosses in a brief protest service against an SADF raid into Botswana a few days earlier. The crosses, each bearing the name of one of the people killed in the raid were erected on four 'graves', where the Black Sash members kept a brief vigil.

Liturgy

One of Diakonia's aims is to link liturgy to social issues, so that faith and life may be integrated.

In the first few years of the organisation, Diakonia held an annual service on 16 December to focus on the need for a new covenant in South Africa.

Since the publication of the Worker Rights Statement in 1983, Diakonia encouraged congregations of member churches to focus on workers on the first Sunday of May, through annual Worker Sunday events. Special liturgies were made available to local churches which could be used to draw attention to the rights of workers.

A number of services were held over the years to focus on the plight of detainees and to protest about deaths in detention. As well as the 1987 Good Friday 'Service for Children in Detention', a second service to pray for detainees was held on 12 June, marking the first anniversary of the national State of Emergency. A large congregation including a number of relatives of detainees, church leaders and consular officials took part in the service, which was held at the Central Methodist Church.

A Christmas 'Service for the Homeless' was held to mark the end of 1987 as the Year of Shelter for the Homeless, and also to make relevant to the current situation the birth of Jesus Christ, who was himself homeless. Diakonia also produced a resource kit to help churches to link their Christmas services with the theme of homelessness.

Churches marching together

I have been asked to share some thoughts on Diakonia's observance of Good Friday. I write against a background of a couple of strokes, a move from one continent to another, and all the ravages of time – 89 this year.

Diakonia's observance of Good Friday was, of course, part of its corporate life, especially that part which we call the spiritual aspect. There are a couple of features which stand out in my mind.

CROSSES TO BEAR ... Bishop Phillip Russell leads the early morning procession on Good Friday

Silent protest march

A SILENT procession of nearly 1 000, led by clergymen carrying symbolic wooden crosses, filed through the early morning streets of Durban on Good Friday.

The march symbolised Christ's crucifixion and resurrection and the recent banning of 18 organisations and a newspaper.

In a second symbolic protest, members of the Black Sash dug four graves and planted crosses on the beach opposite the Natal Command army headquarters to protest against Monday's SADF raid into Botswana.

Archbishop Denis Hurley, the Rev Stanley Magoba, and Bishops Philip Russell and Michael Nuttall led the procession.

Nineteen gagged people carried crosses to protest restrictions on 18 against organisations and the banning of the newspaper New Nation.

1. The clearly ecumenical nature of the activity. One was able to see clergy of all churches sharing in the marches and in the silences.
2. The activities ranged from marching to standing still either to hear someone expounding the nature of Good Friday, or just to listen to the church bell of St Paul's.
3. When all the marching with all that was involved stopped, we were able to gather in an appropriate place – whether it was in the chancel of St Paul's Church or on the steps of the City Hall.
4. The fact that the whole action was for this purpose only. That is to say there was no friendly cup of tea afterwards. When it was over, we went to our own homes, wherever they may be, with the memories of all that had been taking place.

I cannot imagine anyone who was there not wanting to thank God for all that had been arranged by Diakonia but, above all else, to thank God for Jesus Christ and for his death on that Good Friday, so that they look forward with joy to the resurrection.

Archbishop-Emeritus Philip Russell

1988

Black Sash members plant a cross on one of the mock graves on the beach in front of Natal Command

Prayer of Intercession

Heavenly Father, you sent your Son as a servant of the truth. Because that truth ran against the evil in people's hearts, leaders of the people rejected and tried to silence him. Look upon those who suffer now under banning and restrictions. Look upon our whole country where an endeavour is made to silence the truth.

Act of Commitment

Lord Jesus, on this Good Friday
>we remember that your voice was brutally silenced
>by authorities who found your message too threatening.
In our service and procession today
>we have meditated on the pain, agony and humiliation
>you were made to undergo.
We have remembered that the silencing of your voice
>through crucifixion and death
>gave way to the glory of your resurrection
>when your teaching was freed to resound through all time and history.
We have also reflected that
>many voices which stand for justice
>are being silenced in our country.

Each person places their right hand on the shoulder of the person next to them as everyone says:

We commit ourselves to work
>*to ensure that those voices which have been silenced*
>*by restrictions, bannings and detentions*
>*may be heard once again*
>*so that the truth may be known*
>*so that human rights may be protected and promoted*
>*so that justice may be assured for all your people*
>*and so that a true and lasting peace may be achieved.*
Give us the strength and courage
>*that flow from your passion, death and resurrection,*
>*so that we may not falter in this commitment.*
Help us to play our part in ensuring
>*that detention and bannings*
>*are not the end of the story*
>*but may give way to the glorious freedom*
>*that you intend for all your children*
>*through Jesus Christ our Lord.*

ECUMENICAL SERVICE ON THE 1st ANNIVERSARY of the STATE OF EMERGENCY

Central Methodist Church · Durban · 12 June 1987 5.30p.m.

June 12 Service, 1987.

CRUCIFIED FOR THE TRUTH
GOOD FRIDAY SERVICE

24th March 1989 • 6.30am
Central Methodist Church • Aliwal Street • Durban

**Preacher: Bishop
Wilfred Napier** *OFM*
President, S.A. Catholic Bishops' Conference

STANDING FOR THE TRUTH

During a period of intense repression and growing resistance, much work was happening to imagine and plan for a free, democratic society in South Africa, what that should look like and how it should be organised, including some constitutional proposals already on the table. Freedom was somehow in the air, even if not visible on the ground.

At the same time the apartheid government, coming under increasing pressure from internal resistance and external anti-apartheid movements, was acting in contradictory ways – continuing to use detentions, bogus trials and propaganda to intimidate and undermine those working for justice, while secretly beginning to meet and talk with members of the liberation movement, and selectively releasing detainees.

EVALUATION

Diakonia was established to mobilise its member churches to a fuller involvement in the struggle for justice. However, there is a tendency for organisations of this kind to move away from that task because it proves so difficult, and instead to become more directly involved in the struggle for justice on behalf of the churches. This means attending the meetings of community organisations and providing a church link with their campaigns. In itself this was a valuable contribution: the problem was that it was not affecting or changing the church in any significant way.

From Diakonia's analysis of the church, the organisation also became very aware of the struggle going on for the church's life and soul. With monotonous regularity Diakonia was receiving right-wing religious publications informing them how 'nasty' liberation theology was, telling Diakonia about all the 'wicked doings' of organisations like the South African Council of Churches (SACC) and the Institute for Contextual Theology (ICT) and how 'dangerous' it would be to be influenced by 'benighted' church leaders such as Archbishop Tutu.

The church had indeed become a 'site of struggle.'

If organisations like Diakonia neglected their task of mobilising the church for a positive involvement in the struggle for justice, they realised that there were powerful forces energetically mobilising the church for a negative role in that struggle.

Two months of questioning and searching by Diakonia staff and Executive, with clergy, with heads of churches, with community organisations and with trade unions, convinced everyone that a new aim was what the organisation needed. This evaluation process was expertly facilitated by Dr Wolfram Kistner, formerly Director of the SACC's Division of Justice and Reconciliation, Vivienne Taylor of the University of Cape Town's School of Social Work & Administration and Bobby Marie, an Organiser with the National Union of Metalworkers of South Africa (Numsa).

A new aim for Diakonia was accepted at a Council meeting on 7 March 1989.

> *The aim of Diakonia is, in keeping with the demands of the gospel, to work with its member churches in the struggle for a just and democratic South Africa.*

In this context, the theme for the 1989 Good Friday Service was 'Crucified for the Truth.'

Starting at Central Methodist Church, the focus was the plight of detainees and particularly those on hunger strike, the Delmas trialists, and conscientious objectors sentenced to six years in prison.

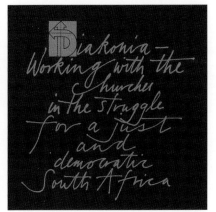

The preacher was Bishop Wilfrid Napier OFM.

The procession of more than 1000 people moved through the streets of Durban to St Paul's Anglican Church led by clergy, religious sisters and heads of church organisations carrying crosses representing those suffering in detention, on trial and in prison.

At St Paul's Church the ritual of flowering the cross was carried out for the first time. The cross of despair and death became, for all those present, a tree of hope and new life.

People committed themselves to stand for the truth and to work for justice and a true and lasting peace. They prayed for help in transforming the cross of pain and humiliation, which so many were suffering in South Africa, into a tree of life, bringing freedom and justice, healing and reconciliation for all people.

PROTEST!

—PICTURES BY—
PATRICK MTOLO
ALAN COXON
GREG KNOWLER

Where angels fear to tread . . . many protesters balanced precariously on a war remembrance statue in Francis Farewell Square during yesterday's protest march through the city centre.

Jam-packed . . . more than 20 000 protesters spanned the length and breadth of West Street yesterday when they marched from Emmanuel Cathedral to the Durban City Hall.

Supporting the struggle . . . Durban's religious leaders — including Catholic Archbishop Denis Hurley (third left) and Anglican Bishop of Natal Michael Nuttall (fourth left) strode arm in arm at the head of the MDM protest march.

'Human rights not human riots' . . . people carrying placards and banners streamed down West Street.

The silent procession of witnesses

Although I had heard of the Diakonia Good Friday procession through the streets of Durban many years before, it was only when I was invited to preach and take part in this special feature of the ecumenical movement in Durban that I got a first-hand taste of its true quality.

The service in the Central Methodist Church was short, sharp and to the point, thus setting the atmosphere and tone for the silent procession of witnesses from the Church to St Paul's Anglican Church. The silent procession was in stark contrast to the other processions or protest marches that Church Leaders were participating in at the time.

So the message was also very different. The Diakonia Good Friday procession was a closer expression of what actually took place on the first Good Friday, from the Garden of Olives, to the Praetorium, through the lanes and by-ways of Jerusalem to Golgotha. There the wood of the Cross was bedecked with the precious body and blood of Jesus as he was crucified.

The Diakonia procession also began in the reflective mood of the Garden, then it emerged into the public arena – the streets of Durban. In later years it culminated in the main square of the city, where all passing by could witness the "flowering of the cross" and its being held aloft in witness to the world of the infinite love and goodness of the Lord.

+ Wilfrid Cardinal Napier OFM
Roman Catholic Archbishop of Durban

Zulu **Mission News**

ARCHDIOCESE OF DURBAN
Archbishop's House
P.O. Box 2184, Durban 4000
Natal South Africa, Telephone: 3010417

An occasional newsletter from the office of Archbishop Denis E. Hurley   JULY 1989

His Grace Archbishop Hurley heads the Good Friday procession carrying the large wooden 'cross of commitment'.

Archbishop Denis Hurley leads ecumenical commitment to building a new South Africa

GOOD FRIDAY
ECUMENICAL SERVICE

Central Methodist Church
Durban
24 March 1989
Theme: Crucified for the Truth

CRUCIFIED FOR THE TRUTH

life of hell   THE TRUTH   DEAD ACTIVIST TO BE SILENCED   MISERY   PUPILS ATTACKED   YOUTH TO HANG   KILLING

Crucified for the Truth – from Despair and Death to Hope and new Life
Extract of sermon by Bishop Wilfrid Napier OFM

1989

Most of us grew up in the belief that to tell the truth and to stand up for the truth is the right thing to do. Our gathering here today is evidence that this is not so! Many of our brothers and sisters have learned the hard way that, under a benighted government or regime, even one which claims to be defending Christian teaching and values, the truth can and does hurt.

At this moment, those for whom this service is being held, the Delmas Four, the Emergency detainees, the banned and restricted, the conscientious objectors in jail or at risk of being jailed, are suffering for the truth, some to the extreme limit.

Truly they are being crucified for the truth.

By all accounts crucifixion was a brutal and horribly painful form of punishment. It was reserved for rebels, slaves and bandits, i.e. for non-citizens and non-persons.

Anyone who has witnessed the effects of detention, solitary confinement, torture – psychological or physical – will readily appreciate the appropriateness of likening such actions to crucifixion. The detainee, the political prisoner, the prisoner of conscience, no less than was the Lord Jesus, is attacked in the very depths of his/her being. They are reduced to the status of non-persons, by being stripped of their fundamental rights – the right to freedom, to their good name, their integrity, their dignity. Their minds as well as their bodies are subjected to shameful torture and degradation. They are truly subjected to crucifixion.

But what has this to do with truth?

Truth in the scriptures, but especially in St John's writing, is the way God wants things to be in relation to Himself and all his creation, in particular humans, to whom he gave special status by creating them in his own image and likeness. So we are speaking about the truth about man/woman, the truth about their dignity and rights which come directly from God's loving act of creation, God's merciful act of redemption and God's renewing act of sanctification. The truth above all is the one who reveals God in his person, his actions and words, i.e. Jesus – God's own revelation.

To the extent then that our brothers and sisters whom we are remembering are associated with Jesus in witnessing to the truth about man/woman, to that extent is their suffering for their God-given rights a sharing in the crucifixion of Jesus.

The suffering of the victims of the present repression is a challenge to the Christian community. More than ever the churches are challenged not to stand at a distance like the disciples, or to go into the wrong company like Peter.

The response of the Christian community to the situation of those whom we are remembering must be to support them in their stand for the truth.

During this service, the cross is to be transformed from being a symbol of despair and death into one of hope and new life. We are all being asked to commit ourselves to bring forth out of the shame and insult of our apartheid past and present the new South Africa of mutual acceptance and love.

As we make our act of commitment to stand for the truth, let us realise that we are binding ourselves to the process of conversion, which may well lead us, too, to accept suffering so that all may eventually be freed from the indignities of discrimination and injustice.

May the suffering of this time bring true freedom and justice, healing and reconciliation to all in our land.

A Prayer for Good Friday

Jesus, you were crucified for the truth.
You talked too much,
    walked with the poor.
You threatened the powerful.
Jealous, eager to protect their privileges
    they killed you.
They are killing us now.

Some among us have been crucified.
Like you, mocked and spat on;
    misunderstood in their own communities,
like you, betrayed by friends,
    tortured, buried in haste.

At Delmas they told the truth.
Workers cry out the truth of their exploitation.
Young men won't fight to defend a lie.
The detained are silent witness:
    the price of truth is high.

You come to bring God's kingdom of justice and peace –
    help us to build it with you.
You come to tell the poor and the outcast of your love –
    open our hearts also.
You come to tell us of the Way, the Truth and the Life –
    teach us to walk your path.

Child of God, you wept in the garden,
faced with the loneliness of your torture and death:
    give us your strength.
Be with all who struggle to build your kingdom,
and help us to live out your truth, all the days of our life.

PEACE THROUGH THE CROSS

Good Friday Ecumenical Service for an end to Natal Violence

Friday 13 April, 1990
6.30 a.m.
Central Methodist Church
Aliwal Street, Durban

PREACHER
Bishop Michael Nuttall

Published by Diakonia, 20 St. Andrews Street, Durban

CHANGE IS COMING!

The year after the 1989 Good Friday service was described by many as a time of surprises. Five series of events stood out:

• A Defiance Campaign which challenged many forms of apartheid, most notably that of beaches and hospitals, as well as restrictions on public demonstrations and marches. What was very striking were the numbers involved and the significant support of the churches, an element that had been largely absent from the Defiance Campaign of 1952.

• The military defeat of South Africa in Angola, which opened the way for negotiations leading to the independence of Namibia.

• The courageous hunger strike by over 600 State of Emergency detainees, which led to their release, under severe restrictions. These restrictions were also defied, so that they became largely meaningless and were lifted along with many other restrictions on 2 February 1990.

• P.W. Botha's stroke, followed by the election of F.W. de Klerk as leader of the National Party and then eventually as State President, and his far-ranging speech of 2 February 1990, which created new freedoms for political movements and possibilities for negotiations.

• The decision of newly-elected State President de Klerk to allow public protest, which led to a series of spectacular protest marches all over South Africa, and gave a very vivid indication of the support enjoyed by the African National Congress (ANC) and the mass democratic movement.

In this context, the state felt compelled to release such long-term prisoners as Walter Sisulu and Ahmed Kathrada – and then some months later Nelson Mandela – creating an unprecedented sense of euphoria and hope.

In Natal all of these events, however, were marred by continuing violence between the ANC, Cosatu, Inkatha YeSizwe and the UDF, which had left close to 4 000 dead in the previous three years, and thousands of others injured or displaced from their homes. Prospects for peace appeared bleak.

THE CHURCH RESPONDS

Both the positive and negative events of the previous year greatly challenged Diakonia and its member churches. The new political climate at a national level challenged Diakonia to re-examine all that they were doing in the light of the greater freedom of political organisations to express the demands of oppressed people. The precise role of the church in this new context and in the future called for thorough discussion.

Violence in Natal had escalated to such an extent that towards the end of 1989 Diakonia decided as an organisation to make the promotion of peace its theme for 1990 and to try to ensure that all programmes and events focussed on this theme.

PEACE PROCESSION

And so in the early morning of Friday 13 April well over 1200 people processed from a service in Central Methodist Church, at which Anglican Bishop Michael Nuttall had preached, through the streets of central Durban to St Paul's Anglican Church, praying for an end to the violence in Natal.

At the head of the procession a number of church leaders, including Ms Virginia Gcabashe, first vice-president of the SACC, took turns in carrying a large cross made of the charred roof beams from a house in Ntuzuma burned down by a petrol bomb.

The theme for the service was *'Peace through the Cross.'* As a symbol of commitment to working for peace, each participant carried a small individual cross during the procession. Many took part in the special flowering of the cross ceremony to symbolise their commitment to working for peace and transformation.

Later in the day the large cross which had led the procession was taken back to the township of Ntuzuma, where it was used in the Good Friday service at the Roman Catholic Church of St Paul. As the charred cross made from beams from their own homes was brought in, many residents were in tears.

After the service the cross was carried in procession to the boundary between Ntuzuma and Lindelani, where it was 'planted' as a sign of peace between these two areas, which had been in conflict for more than a year. A year later the cross remained in position: there had been no further outbreak of violence between the two areas.

PEACE · 1990

The Holy Spirit rains down blessings

My first experience of the Diakonia Good Friday service was on 13th April 1990. I recall being drawn to this service by the fact that the cross which was paraded through the streets of Durban in silence was made from the burnt-out door frames of a home, in the height of apartheid violence. This I believe to be the very beginning of God's awakening in me to the injustices of our society in South Africa. My Christian journey was still brand new in the area of social justice issues, both in a real sense and from a Christian perspective.

It was a number of years later that I became involved in my second experience of this service under the leadership of the Revd Carol Walsh, when I was asked to set up prayer stations at the City Hall steps for prayers for healing with people. This experience, too, further helped my growth in crossing the barriers and praying with people from all walks of life, encountering the deep pain many lived with.

For the past three years, as a Diakonia Council member for the Methodist Church, I have been involved in the planning of this service with staff and people from different denominations. This experience has blessed me beyond measure and added to my journey in so many ways.

The most recent moment was in 2008 on the City Hall steps, handing out the flowers to people as the rain fell gently down. It was as if the Holy Spirit of God was raining down on the City of Durban and its people. A complete moment of blessing and overwhelming joy came when I helped lift the base of the beautifully flowered cross into its stand.

To God be all the glory for the things he has done and will continue to do in and through this service and his people who faithfully serve him!

Janice Wahl

Litany

Lord, you want us to be a new people committed to your peace and justice. Open our hearts and lives to

Peace through the Cross.

Jesus, you confronted the intolerance of the Pharisees and the Roman rulers. May your Spirit break down our own fortresses of intolerance and those which beset our land. May we together know

Peace through the Cross.

Jesus, although you were a Jew, you spoke to the Samaritan woman at the well, thereby challenging the apartheid of your day. Strengthen us in our work against the apartheid of our time, so that there may be

Peace through the Cross.

Jesus, in the Garden of Gethsemane, you overcame the darkness of fear. In our struggle for justice, conquer our fears with the power of your love, so that our land may experience

Peace through the Cross.

Jesus, you despised the arrogance of wealth and power, and embodied the way of the suffering servant. In our pursuit of dignity for all people, may we shun the arrogance which separates people from each other, and allow you to bring

Peace through the Cross.

Jesus, at your arrest you said that those who live by the sword will die by the sword, and you commanded your disciples to put away their weapons. Deliver us from the self-destructive grip of aggression, so that we may have

Peace through the Cross.

Jesus, as a brother and friend, you yourself suffered poverty and brought hope, life and dignity to the poor. By your Spirit, empower the poor of South Africa and, with them, may all know

Peace through the Cross.

Lord Jesus, today we worship you, the Prince of Peace, and we give all of ourselves to you in praise and prayer. May our worship today be a time of shared faith, of renewed commitment and of hope restored. May we, this Good Friday, affirm with one voice that there can only be

Peace through the Cross.

A teenager walks past the cross at the boundary of Ntuzuma and Lindelani.
Pic: John Woodroof

'Cross of Peace' bridges township border

Mdu Lembede

A WOODEN cross made of charred roof beams from a petrol-bombed house was planted at the boundary of the Lindelani squatter settlement and Ntuzuma, to indicate the residents' desire for lasting peace in the area.

Residents from both sides carried the cross in a procession after a Good Friday mass held at night, at the nearby Roman Catholic Church.

The cross was planted as a symbol to all who suffered when violence broke out in the area in December. Many lives were lost, and about 90 houses were gutted.

During the day on Friday, residents from the area joined more than 1 000 people who took part in a "procession for peace" through the streets of central Durban.

The procession, from the Central Methodist Church to the St Paul's Anglican Church, was part of the annual inter-denominational Good Friday service arranged by Diakonia church agency.

The theme of the service this year was "Peace through the Cross".

Good Friday Service

Healed by the Cross

Organised by: Diakonia and Durban & District Council of Churches

'By his wounds we have been healed' Is. 53:5

Central Methodist Church
Aliwal Street, Durban
29 March 1991 6.30am
Sermon: Sheena Duncan
SACC Vice-President

Published by Diakonia, 20 St Andrews St, Durban, 4001. Production by Media Design Services, PO Box 1943, Hillcrest, 3650.

HOPE AND DISAPPOINTMENT

Much of the year between April 1990 and March 1991 was characterised by frustrating disappointments, as the national 'talks about talks' seemed constantly to be at risk of collapsing.

Hopes and high expectations were not met, and indemnity for exiles was not granted by the government. Exiles were therefore unable to return, and so the ANC could not hold its conference – a crucial preliminary step before genuine negotiations could start. Political violence did not end, but escalated, with some of the worst incidents flowing from the conflict between the ANC and Inkatha spreading to the Transvaal.

In this difficult climate, Diakonia continued to promote the theme chosen for 1990: *'Working for Peace in Natal'*, and may have played some small part in gradually developing a better climate for peace.

Eventually the ANC and the recently-formed Inkatha Freedom Party (IFP) were able to meet at top level under the leadership of Nelson Mandela and Chief Mangosuthu Buthelezi on 29 January 1991 and reaffirmed on 18 February that *'our two organisations ... are at peace'*, although even this did not lead to a cessation of violence. In fact the *'Peace Accord'* was extremely fragile and needed a systematic process of communication, implementation and monitoring.

'HEAL, RECONCILE, BUILD'

Diakonia's theme for 1991 was *'Heal, Reconcile, Build'*, following on the previous year's theme.

The 1991 Good Friday service and procession through the streets of Durban had, by now, become a keenly-anticipated annual event. Year by year more and more people were participating in what had become a major ecumenical gathering.

1991 saw an estimated 1500 people assembling at Central Methodist Church at 6.30am on Good Friday morning, worshipping together, hearing the inspiring sermon of Sheena Duncan, SACC vice-president, and then processing solemnly to St Paul's Anglican Church, and celebrating the culmination of the worship as the promise of Easter was declared symbolically by song and dance, flowers and prayer.

The theme of the service was *'Healed by the Cross'*, focussing on one of the words of the year's theme. Its purpose was to pray for healing in South Africa.

A large cross had been painted by well-known artist

DANCERS from the Anglican diocese of Natal perform a ritual dance around the cross, brightly adorned with symbols of healing, during yesterday's Good Friday ecumenical service, which had the theme "Healed by the Cross".

D.N. 25/3/91

FORGIVENESS THE THEME AT ECUMENICAL DAWN SERVICE

Saturday News Reporter

A BIGGER congregation than ever attended Durban's annual Good Friday ecumenical dawn service, which focused attention on the need for healing and reconciliation in strife-torn South Africa and particularly in Natal.

The congregation walked in procession from the Central Methodist Church to St Paul's Anglican Church, the impressive line-up stretching for more than a city block.

Mr Paddy Kearney, director of Diakonia church agency, said at the start of the service that if there was to be a new South Africa, there would have to be forgiveness and healing.

"We can't be surprised that there are many people who are bitter, angry and hostile because of what has happened to their family or friends, because of what has happened to themselves and their own homes."

He said: "Forgiveness and healing seem quite impossible from a human viewpoint.

"That is why we are here today, because in the Cross we can see a powerful source of forgiveness and healing."

The sermon was preached by Mrs Sheena Duncan, senior vice-president of the South African Council of Churches, and the procession was led by top Natal clergymen.

Dina Cormick with scenes representing the pain and suffering in the Natal violence being transformed into healing and reconstruction. Veiled in mourning purple, it was carried through the streets by church leaders as a single bell tolled the death of a monarch.

As the cross was unveiled and surrounded by flowers at St Paul's, suddenly the assurance of eventual peace and healing shone on the faces of the congregation. It was a most moving moment.

The beautiful *'Cross of Healing'* was placed on the wall of the Justice Hall at the Ecumenical Centre, as it was then called, where visitors could see it. It now stands in the entrance to the Diakonia Council of Churches' offices in the re-named Diakonia Centre, and is much admired as it tells a poignant story of a unique period in the history of this province – and the church's involvement in bringing healing and peace.

Focus of Durban prayers to be on Natal violence

NEW NATION 28/3/91

Diakonia and the Durban District Council of Churches are jointly organising an ecumenical service to be held on Good Friday under the theme "Healed by the Cross".

The purpose of the service will be to pray for healing and reconciliation in South Africa after long years of apartheid and the four-years old Natal violence.

Among those who will be hosting the service are Bishop Stanley Mogoba, Presiding Bishop of the Methodist Church, Archbishop Denis Hurley of the Catholic Church, Bishop Michael Nuttal of the Anglican Church, Bishop Norman Hudson of the Methodist Church and Rev Sam Khumalo of the Presbyterian Church of Africa.

The sermon will be delivered by Sheena Duncan, vice President of the South African Council of Churches.

The service at the Central Methodist Church will be followed by a solemn street procession in which a large wooden cross will be carried aloft while a single bell will toll.

The cross has been painted with symbols of healing by a well-known Durban artist Dina Cormick.

Unveiling

The procession will end at St Paul's Anglican Church, next to the Central Post Office, where the cross will be unveiled and decorated with flowers.

A team of dancers from the Anglican Diocese of Natal will then perform a ritual dance around the cross.

The congregation will then commit themselves to work for healing and reconciliation.

All those participating in the service will receive a small cross as a memento of the occasion.

"To be people of faith in times of doubt."

I am not sure of the year this song was sung at the end of the Good Friday procession, but it has moved and followed me ever since. Perhaps because its simple, yet rousing melody reminded me of an old church song, perhaps it just fitted my mood at the time – tired of racism, yet uplifted by the multi-ethnic crowd singing it; anxious about further police action against informal settlers on the banks of the N2, yet assured that there would be a time when dignity was restored.

I just remember the longing spirit, the vulnerability of it all – but isn't that also the motor of all creativity, of all inspiration? So often – after the service and the flowering of the cross – I would drive back to Reservoir Hills, my car filled with congregants of St John's Lutheran Church, where we then would continue with worship in our little church, and the pictures, songs and sights of the early morning procession would keep on playing in our minds and prayers.

Yes, God's peace is fragile – like a treasure in earthen vessels (2 Cor.6:12). But the light of the gospel shines on, perhaps through the brokenness and fragility of it all.

"Blessed are the cracked, they let the light through", I once read on the exhibition board of an emergency and trauma unit of a large South African hospital ward. It was placed there by a surgeon who fought with the daily problems with apartheid laws, health policy, police brutality, fighting factions. Often enough his help had come too late. He suffered from the feelings of helplessness. That's why he had put the *"Blessed"* saying up on the wall to always remind himself that his work made sense despite the greatest adversity.

To me the song with the words of the prayer attributed to St. Francis do the very same – they are a light in a dark place; they show me what is real beyond all doubt: God's wonderful grace that wins the day, giving me a glimpse of God's justice, healing and forgiveness here and now.

Revd Klaus J. Burckhardt
Dept. of Peace & Justice
Ev.-luth. Church of Hannover, Germany

Good Friday Ecumenical Service

Healed by the Cross

'By his wounds
we have been healed'
Is. 53:5

Central Methodist Church, Durban
29 March 1991 6.30am
Sermon: Sheena Duncan
SACC Senior Vice-President

Organized by Diakonia and the Durban & District Council of Churches

Heal, reconcile, build
Extract of sermon by Sheena Duncan, SACC Vice President

Some of the participants at the service.

Diakonia's theme for this year is *'Heal, reconcile, build.'*

We are overwhelmed by the task before us. Everywhere we look we are confronted by destruction and suffering, death and woundedness. As I wrote this, news came of 15 more people brutally killed at a funeral vigil in Alexandra. There are so many thousands of people who mourn their dead and whose sorrow has to be borne somehow. Each death now seems to lead to other deaths. Each day brings new tragic events which we cannot begin to understand. There are so many thousands of people who are consumed with hatred and anger, whose souls and spirits are deeply wounded by these destructive emotions. Families, communities, the whole society is broken and disordered.

So, here we are, a people in exile from the kingdom of God, seeking to find our way home to where justice and peace are to be found. We are a people who are afraid. We know that our adversary, the devil *"as a roaring lion walketh about seeking whom he may devour."* We know in our inmost being the despair which led Jesus on the cross to cry: *"My God, my God, why did you abandon me?"* But yet we also know that God is the Lord of history. We too, like the people of Judah in exile in Babylon, ask in wonder and incomprehension: *"Who could have seen the Lord's hand in this?"* Which of us can see the Lord's hand in all this?

In our short time on earth, we, homo sapiens made in the image of God, have almost managed to destroy God's creation, plundering the earth, polluting the waters, blotting out the sun, killing children from hunger and disease. God made us in God's image, but we have so distorted the image and misused the creation that we are indeed in danger of being cast into outer darkness. But yet, Jesus Christ was born. We are lost in wonder, love and praise as we contemplate this incredible purpose which has created and redeemed us; which makes us meaningful in the whole vast universe which God created. We can indeed see the Lord's hand in this.

As we carry this cross through the streets of Durban today, we do so in anguish and sorrow for our sins. For our responsibility for the exiles, the beaten, the poor, the oppressed. But with them we know that we are God's co-creators. That we are given the power to heal, reconcile and build. We know that God has a purpose for us. We know that our peace is only to be found in doing that purpose. We know that the joy of the resurrection is upon us. We know that we too will one day sing and shout for joy in the streets of Jerusalem. We know that we will go out from this place in the power of the Holy Spirit to live and work to His praise and glory. So be it.

To be people of faith in times of doubt

Refrain: To be people of faith in times of doubt,
to be people of hope in times of despair,
to be people of peace, people of peace,
O Lord, your instruments of peace.

Where we encounter hatred let us bring your love;
Where hurt has been oppressive, your healing care;
Wherever there are people who are needing to be free;
Make your Church an instrument of peace.

To heal the broken-hearted, to comfort those who mourn,
To go to those imprisoned, bring freedom to the bound;
To be a light for all who struggle to be free;
Make your Church an instrument of peace.

In giving to the hungry, in satisfying thirst,
In welcoming the stranger, in comforting the ill;
In being those who hunger for justice and for truth;
Make us all your instruments of peace.

Painted Easter cross brings a message of hope and reconciliation to strife-torn Natal

Myrtle Ryan

THE cross which will be carried in the Good Friday Ecumenical Service in Durban is vivid not only in colour but in hope.

Based on a South American concept of painted crosses showing the oppressed and injured receiving solace from Jesus, it depicts the scars and wounds of the Natal violence. But it's theme, *Healed By The Cross*, is that of a better future.

Durban artist Dina Cormick, commissioned to paint the cross, said she had given much thought to the concept. "At the bottom lies an overturned, burning bus which has been shot at. The injured make their way upwards to the centre of the cross-arms where Jesus is healing people. From each arm they stream — those fleeing the flames of a burning house, the injured, sick and despondent. It all culminates in triumph at the top where a group of workers are hard at work on a building — building for peace," she says. "There are also several trees. Trees are great healers. And a river of life runs through the scenes."

The service commences at 6.30am on Friday at the central Methodist Church and the procession, led by Archbishop Denis Hurley, Bishop Michael Nuttall and Bishop Stanley Mogoba, will make its way to St Paul's Anglican Cathedral.

The cross will be draped in purple and only unveiled at St Paul's Church.

Dina Cormick puts the finishing touches to the cross.
Picture: Sherelee Clarke

People will be invited to place flowers at its foot and Anglicans from all over the Diocese of Natal will dance around the cross.

Everyone who attends the service will be given their own small cross with a linocut screenprint by Dina Cormick on it to carry during the procession.

GOOD FRIDAY ECUMENICAL SERVICE

Central Methodist Church · Aliwal Street, Durban

17th April 1992 · 6.30 am

SERMON: Di Oliver
Natal Crisis Committee

Organised by Diakonia and the Durban & District Council of Churches

A YEAR OF CONTRADICTIONS

Plans for peace and conspiracies of violence. Increasing poverty and unemployment amidst prospects of growing trade and wealth. Negotiations for democracy but continuing top-down state autocracy. Closing of schools and sacking of teachers while millions went uneducated. Shack-dwellers hounded and harassed as luxurious office blocks stood half-empty. AIDS on the increase while medical costs soared. Expensive restaurants full every day while food prices spiralled out of control and millions starved.

As South Africa moved into its 'transition', the sense of living in a third-world country increased day by day. The symptoms were all there: increasing disparity between the rich and the poor; little accountability of most political figures to the ordinary people; marginalisation of the poorest and most deprived; high walls and armed guards around upper-class neighbourhoods; plentiful supplies of arms and ammunition; roaming bands of vigilantes killing the innocent and destroying homes; assassinations of those working for peace and democracy.

Yet the year from March 1991 saw many signs of hope.

The first conference of the ANC inside South Africa for thirty years took place. Twenty-three political groupings and organisations attended a Peace Convention and signed a National Peace Accord, setting up structures to deal with and counter the terrible violence which continued to take an awesome toll. The Convention for a Democratic South Africa (CODESA) gathered most of the significant political groupings together to start a process of negotiations to lead to a new South Africa.

Grassroots people made their views known, taking to the streets in their thousands demanding the freeing of all political prisoners, protesting the imposition of Value Added Tax (VAT) and demonstrating against the opening of yet another tricameral parliament. An estimated eighty percent of South Africa's work force took part in a two-day stay-away in November, giving impetus to the calls by organised workers for a say in the restructuring of South Africa's economy to the benefit of all, not only the rich.

However, some of the signs of hope revealed their darker side almost immediately.

The Land Acts, the Group Areas Act and the Population Registration Act were repealed. Everyone thought the final legal pillars of apartheid had been destroyed. Until white men found they were still being conscripted into an apartheid army. And black people trying to move to a better place to live found economic apartheid replacing racial apartheid.

Right-wing violence became more overt, with bomb blasts, random shootings and open confrontations joining the increasing evidence of the involvement of some security force members in the so-called 'third force', orchestrating harassment, assassinations and violent attacks, carefully selected to trigger off further spirals of revenge and counter-attack.

Throughout the year, the church increasingly let its voice be heard at a national and regional level. Church leaders took strong initiatives for peace and justice, sometimes very publicly, but often quietly and unobtrusively. Acting as the conscience of the nation, they contributed significantly to the setting up of the Peace Convention, and continued to act in the structures set up by the National Peace Accord.

Against this backdrop, Diakonia persevered with its work for peace, justice and reconciliation. It was a difficult year for most people in the country: the gleams of light that shone through the dark clouds helped to illuminate the path onwards towards a just and democratic South Africa.

SUFFERING, RECONCILIATION, PEACE

The Good Friday service on 17 April 1992 was jointly organised with the Durban & District Council of Churches (DDCC). More than 1500 people attended. During a brief service at Central Methodist Church, Di Oliver preached eloquently on the theme. Those who knew something of Di's history were particularly moved by the insights that her own suffering had brought to her.

The procession then moved through the streets to St Paul's Anglican Church. This year women carried the cross, made from the charred timber of a home burned down in the violence. They included women from Uganda, an informal settlement at Umlazi where women and children had recently been shot dead by warlords. Others carrying the cross were two returned exiles, church leaders, and community leaders who had worked with the community of KwaNqetho to bring about peace in that area.

When the cross was lifted up at St Paul's, transformed by the beauty of flowers and foliage, the symbolism of good coming out of evil, and peace out of suffering, was striking. Prayer cards were distributed as a symbol for people to take to their homes.

Through suffering to reconciliation and peace

Extract of sermon by Di Oliver, Natal Crisis Committee

A few years ago I saw a film about Christ's last days on earth. It portrayed the crucifixion: driving the nails into Christ's hands; hammering the nails into Christ's feet; forcing the thorn-crown mockingly onto Christ's head; the beauty of that human form beaten, broken, bleeding.

It is an image that has remained with me – like the image of a child's body being borne in the arms of friends in Soweto in 1976; like the image of a mother and baby tied to her back, gunned down in Umlazi last month; like the image of a charred human frame draped over the bonnet of a burnt-out car in Alexandra just the other day.

There are many powerful images to help us to reflect on the meaning of this day in our journey of faith.

We come to this day deeply conscious of the suffering in this city, this province, our country. We come looking for answers. Why, Lord, if you suffered so much, if you had to bear the cross of shame, if you died that we might have life in all its fullness, why do we have to bear so much now? Isn't it enough? Have the years of legal apartheid not been enough? Must we see people turning their alienation, their anger, their insecurity, their dispossession on each other, even more so now?

I came to live in this city eighteen months ago. It was hard to leave Table Mountain, the vineyards, the white sand on Fish Hoek beach, St George's Cathedral.

The first six months of living here were uneasy. The violent crime was devastating; the violence was so tangible, so visible, so close, so real; the indifference of the daily press, the people on the streets, in the shops, was disturbing, but so real.

Then I saw advertised that Durban would have an ecumenical service on Good Friday at 6.30am. When I arrived at 6.25am this church was packed. It was the richest variety of people I had seen together for a long time. The crowd straddled the great divides in our society – poor, rich; rural, urban; people of different races, cultures, denominations, speaking different languages, and women taking their place as members of the church leadership. There was a poignancy in the consciousness of having come together on this day – to bear witness together as a Christian community to the sacrifice and death of our beloved Lord in a context that cried out for relief from suffering, death, destruction, selfishness, indifference, fear.

There are no easy answers to the questions that must be ours at this time. But there is something so powerful in the relatedness between death and suffering and the life we are called to live as people who believe that Christ died for us. Something grows in us when we are faced with our own mortality because of the death of those close to us. Like Christ, we question – why me, Lord, why us, why Durban, Umlazi, Imbali?

We are told in St John's Gospel (12:27/28) that, faced with death, our Lord said: *"Now my soul is troubled. And what should I say – 'Please save me from this hour?'"* But, unlike us so often, this isn't where the prayer ended. In pain, and surely anguish and fear, Jesus goes on to say: *"No, it is for this reason that I have come to this hour of suffering. God, glorify your name."*

The possibilities for reconciliation and peace depend on us. The promise of the cross is that the suffering will be transformed into reconciliation and peace when we act upon the realisation that it depends upon us to live and work for God's kingdom on earth.

GOOD FRIDAY SERVICE

SUFFERING · RECONCILIATION · PEACE

Central Methodist Church · Aliwal Street, Durban
17th April 1992 · 6.30 am

PEACE

RECONCILIATION

SUFFERING

SERMON: Di Oliver
Natal Crisis Committee

Supporting the oppressed

We have attended the Good Friday services from their inception when a small group of us gathered at dawn to commemorate the death of Christ. In those days, when our parishes were not very integrated, we loved the fact that we could worship with people of different races and creeds. It was wonderful to be 'normal' and not to be divided by the laws of the time.

Because, each year, the theme was carefully planned and pinpointed a pressing human rights issue, we felt it was a way of supporting the oppressed and voicing that support as a group. It made us feel hopeful and it was encouraging to be with like-minded people. In the days when the security police were waiting with their water cannons as we left Central Methodist Church, it strengthened our resolve to stand together for change.

I was very fortunate to be involved in helping with the flowering of the cross. We relied heavily on hope and trust that whatever device we had fitted to the cross to hold the flowers would manage to stay up and not collapse! We would hold our breath as the cross was raised and be elated with relief and joy when all was well. We were filled with the hope that the flowered cross offered.

Our children used to attend the services with us and we would always plan our Easter holidays around the service, only leaving after we had attended. Because it is so meaningful to us, that is still our habit to this day. Now, our grandchildren attend with us and we invariably leave the service reminiscing on the old days, and with renewed hope that together we can change our world.

Marylyn Cason

The Diakonia Community

A Newsletter for Members and Friends June 1992

Strong support at Good Friday Service

THE Diakonia Good Friday Service has become an annual service of significance in the city of Durban. The fact that this is an ecumenical service has helped it to gain widespread popularity.

This year's service was held on Friday 17 April. More than 1 500 people from the Durban functional region attended, which included a large number of people from the townships.

The first venue was the Central Methodist church and, after a brief service, the procession went from there to St. Paul's Anglican Church.

This year women carried a cross, made from the charred timber of a home burnt down in the violence, through the streets of Durban.

Volunteers included women from Uganda (an informal settlement at Umlazi, where women and children were recently shot dead by warlords), two returnees, church leaders and community leaders who have worked with the community of KwaNaqetho (Hillcrest) to bring about peace in that area.

Three theme banners: 'Suffering', 'Reconciliation', 'Peace', were displayed during the solemn procession through the streets.

The service theme was 'Suffering, Reconciliation, Peace'. The preacher was Di Oliver, Secretary of the Natal Crisis Fund, who spoke about her experience of living in a violence

Above: The second half of Diakonia's Good Friday Service was conducted in St. Paul's Anglican Church.

orientated area, and also staying with a family which has been victimised by violence.

At St. Paul's there was a ceremony for 'flowering the cross' in which people were invited to take part.

At the end of the service prayer cards were distributed as a symbol for people to take to their homes.

The flowered cross was later placed in the grounds of the Ecumenical Centre.

DIAKONIA COMMISSIONING SERVICE

SUNDAY 21 JUNE 1992
2.30 pm

Creed of Hope

In the midst of hunger and war
  we celebrate the promise of plenty and peace.
In the midst of oppression and tyranny
  we celebrate the promise of service and freedom.
In the midst of doubt and despair
  we celebrate the promise of faith and hope.
In the midst of fear and betrayal
  we celebrate the promise of joy and loyalty.
In the midst of hatred and death
  we celebrate the promise of love and life.
In the midst of sin and decay
  we celebrate the promise of salvation and renewal.
In contemplation of the dying Lord
  we celebrate the promise of the living Christ.

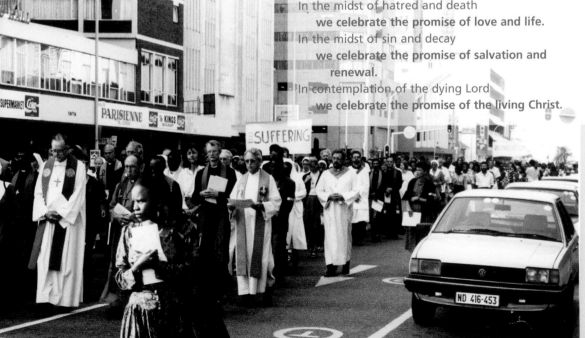

Brought together by the cross · Sihlanganiswe yisiphambano

GOOD FRIDAY SERVICE

Central Methodist Church, Aliwal Street, Durban
9th April 1993 · 6.30 a.m.

Sermon: **Dean Simon Farisani**
Northern Diocese, *ELCSA*

"But now in Christ Jesus you that used to be so far apart from us have been brought very close, by the blood of Christ". Eph. 2:13

"Kepha manje kuKristu uJesu nina enanikade nikude senenziwe abaseduze ngegazi likaKristu" Eph. 2:13

A YEAR OF DISILLUSIONMENT AND VIOLENCE

Nineteen ninety two was a sobering year. The National Peace Accord signed in September the previous year had failed dismally to deliver peace. The CODESA talks which began with a flourish were in tatters within months. There followed a time of escalating violence and profound disillusionment with politicians of all parties. They seemed unwilling to accept responsibility for the violence and reluctant to display the leadership that could resolve the crisis about stalled negotiations.

The year would also be remembered for startling revelations of corruption and mismanagement within state and homeland administrations. In addition, covert activities of the police force and military intelligence were exposed. But, as had become customary in South Africa, the politicians vehemently denied any knowledge and responsibility. In many cases the officials concerned were allowed to retire with golden handshakes and substantial pensions, much to public astonishment and disgust.

Violence continued unabated, a symptom of third force determination to prevent real change, of the ANC/IFP power struggle in Natal, of massive poverty, growing unemployment and lack of housing.

An overwhelming 'yes' vote in the March referendum led to President de Klerk overplaying his hand in the CODESA talks and displaying a *kragdadigheid* (obstinacy) reminiscent of his predecessor P.W. Botha. This attitude, coupled with the Boipatong massacre in June, was the catalyst for the ANC's withdrawal from the negotiations process and presenting the government with 14 pre-conditions for further talks.

There followed in August a programme of mass action by the ANC-Cosatu-South African Communist Party (SACP) alliance for the second half of the year. Business and labour came together to pressurise government to respond positively to the ANC's demands. When the government responded with a hardline approach, the intervention of church leaders brought a lowering of the political temperature and ensured that the general strike took place with minimal violence.

September brought the Ciskei massacre, which showed how disastrous confrontation could be in the current tinder box atmosphere that characterised many parts of South Africa.

The government's eventual response to the pressure of mass action was to hold bilateral talks with the ANC reaching a Record of Understanding on an elected constituent assembly and action on political prisoners, weapons and hostels.

Chief Mangosuthu Buthelezi and the IFP were indignant at this agreement, and linked with Bophutatswana, Ciskei and the Conservative Party to form the Concerned South African Group (Cosag), an unlikely alliance to help homeland leaders and conservative white interests hold onto some power. Chief Buthelezi's constitutional proposals for a separate state of KwaZulu, announced in December, was a further warning of the possible consequences of too close a rapprochement between Pretoria and the ANC if other parties felt decisions were being made for them.

The effect of the ANC's response to the government's post-referendum *kragdadigheid* and KwaZulu's response to ANC/government bilateral agreements made it seem that negotiations would be permanently logjammed by party political posturing.

Sobriety was to come from an unexpected quarter. During the year a growing number of political leaders became increasingly aware that the economy was in a critical state and that, unless the negotiations impasse was resolved speedily, any new government would inherit a ruined economy. That sense of sober realism seemed to help the revival of a multi-party negotiating forum.

A second source of greater realism was the international backdrop provided by events in Bosnia and Angola, highlighting the need to take seriously the existence of ethnic conflicts – the latter showing that elections would not in themselves provide a magic end to conflict. The causes of conflict needed to be dealt with.

Towards the end of the year, there were two small rays of hope that the violence could be brought under control. Coordinated local and international efforts to monitor the violence, though still on a very inadequate scale, had begun to make a difference. There was also a new and growing awareness that traditional leaders could not be cast aside, but had to be respected, persuaded to return to their proper role of leading all their people whatever their political persuasion, and encouraged to involve themselves fully in Peace Accord structures. This new approach bore fruit especially in the South Coast area of Natal.

Perhaps the church also had a more sober view of its own position. Having done everything possible to lay the basis for the National Peace Accord which led to CODESA, the church was largely left on the sidelines to watch both initiatives flounder, at enormous cost to human life, further polarised relationships and economic deterioration. Clearly a more dynamic involvement of the church was needed to ensure that 1993 would not be another 'lost year'. Through involvement in the peace process, in education for democracy and in the massive task of reconstruction that lay ahead, Diakonia planned to be fully part of this more dynamic involvement.

Yet the events unleashed by the tragic assassination of Chris Hani on Saturday 10 April, the day after the Good Friday service, showed once again how delicate and vulnerable the process was.

BROUGHT TOGETHER BY THE CROSS

Durban's eighth ecumenical Good Friday service on 9 April 1993, once again jointly organised by Diakonia and the DDCC, was attended by more than 1500 people from every corner of Durban, as well as from other parts of South Africa and overseas.

Bishop Stanley Mogoba preached at the service in Central Methodist Church.

Many shared in carrying the cross through the streets, including the Daughters of Charity, founded by Mother Theresa, who had recently arrived in Durban to serve the poorest here.

For the first time the painted cross depicting Jesus' suffering and that of the people of Natal, was set up in front of the City Hall instead of at St Paul's Church. This venue was chosen for the final part of the service because it could accommodate a much bigger crowd.

People flocked to decorate the cross with flowers as a sign of their willingness to work for the transformation of society, and as a symbol of hope and resurrection even in the midst of violence, grief and death.

A particularly moving moment was when a group of mourning families arrived from Port Shepstone. They had been bereaved a few days earlier by an attack in which ten young people had been killed. These grieving families each received a cross from Archbishop Wilfrid Napier or Archbishop Denis Hurley.

1993

Confession

We confess, Lord, that we have often seen our neighbours as enemies, rather than as our sisters and brothers for whom you died on the cross.

    Lord have mercy

We confess, Lord, that, while we reverence your cross in our churches, we often fail to see you in those who are crucified by unjust structures and by our cruelty or indifference.

    Christ have mercy

We confess, Lord, that we often lose hope of making peace and fail to use the power that flows from your death and resurrection.

    Lord have mercy

Prayers for reconciliation

Across the barriers that divide race from race
    Reconcile us, O Christ, by your cross.
Across the barriers that divide the rich from the poor
    Reconcile us, O Christ, by your cross.
Across the barriers that divide people of different political views
    Reconcile us, O Christ, by your cross
Across the barriers that divide people of different faiths
    Reconcile us, O Christ, by your cross
Across the barriers that divide Christians
    Reconcile us, O Christ, by your cross
Across the barriers that divide men and women, young and old
    Reconcile us, O Christ, by your cross

EZEBANDLA

ENKONZWENI yamabandla esiwuphawu lukaGudi enhliziyweni yeTheku, lapho kuye kuthwalwe ngokushintshana isiphambano, kube nomunyu omkhulu ngenkathi amakhosikazi ashonelwe esibhicongweni sokubulawa kwabasePort Shepstone. Abashonelwe banikezwe iziphambano ezimhlophe ngabaßhishobhi o-Archbishop Wilfrid Napier noArchbishop Denis Hurley.

One new people: Isizwe Esisha Esimunye

GOOD FRIDAY SERVICE

FOR PEACEFUL ELECTIONS
UKHETHO OLUNOKUTHULA

Emmanuel Cathedral, Durban
1 April 1994, 6.30 am
Sermon : Dr Beyers Naudé

"With His own body Christ broke down the wall that separated them...to create out of the two races *One New People*"

"Ngomzimba wakhe uKrestu wadiliza udonga olubahlukanisayo...ukuba akhe phakathi kwezinhlanga ezimbili *isizwe esisha esimunye*"

Ephesians 2 : 14, 15

JOSTLING FOR POWER

The months after the previous Good Friday service in April 1993 were a difficult period in South Africa's transition. Yet their most striking feature was that negotiations did not break down completely at any point. Great credit was due to all parties for persevering in trying to find an inclusive settlement.

The mass demonstrations which followed the assassination of SACP general secretary, Chris Hani, on 10 April 1993, the day after the Good Friday service, led to the Afrikaner Volksfront being established under the leadership of retired general Constand Viljoen, who later surprised many by his willingness to negotiate with the ANC.

The decision by 19 of the 26 parties in the resumed multi-party negotiations to set 27 April 1994 as the date for the first non-racial general election led to the Conservative Party (CP) and the IFP walking out, amid talk of civil war and bloodshed. Bilateral meetings between the CP and the IFP on the one hand and the government and the ANC on the other, nevertheless continued without interruption.

The publication of the first draft of the Interim Constitution, however, worsened the situation from the viewpoint of those minority parties who said that it had many flaws, especially its failure to entrench regional powers – powers they perceived as their only chance of political survival.

The adoption of the Transitional Executive Council Bill by the multi-party forum in early September further isolated the CP and the IFP. They then transformed their link with the Ciskei and Bophutatswana – previously known as the Concerned South Africa Group (Cosag) – into the Freedom Alliance (FA) in October, to tighten the group's opposition to the agreements being reached in the multi-party forum. However, the involvement of the Afrikaner Weerstand Beweging (AWB) in the FA disturbed many black supporters of the FA and led to this alliance remaining weak.

The Interim Constitution was finalised by the multi-party forum in November without the approval of the FA, and ratified by the tricameral parliament on 22 December.

There were greatly increased anxieties especially in KwaZulu and Natal because of statements by King Goodwill Zwelithini that suggested he would proclaim an independent Zulu Kingdom rather than encourage his people to take part in the April election. There was an alarming increase in war talk and great difficulties were experienced in trying to promote free political activity and voter education in vast areas of KwaZulu and Natal. Political violence escalated on the Reef and in Natal. It was an anxious time for all who were longing for a democratic resolution to this region's problems.

PRAYING FOR THE ELECTIONS

An estimated three thousand people came together on 1 April for the Good Friday service and procession, to mourn the deaths of more than 8 000 people in political violence in Natal and to express their desire for a free, fair and peaceful election due to be held three weeks later, as well as to underline their wish for unity as *'one new people.'* Emmanuel Cathedral was packed to capacity, with many crammed in the courtyard outside.

To emphasise the peace theme of the service, burned beams from strife-torn Bhambayi, an informal settlement outside Durban, were used to make a cross. The two pieces came from gutted houses in the so-called 'green' and 'red' areas of the settlement to create a cross of hope and unity.

The sermon preached by the Revd Dr Beyers Naudé, former General Secretary of the SACC, challenged the congregation to support efforts for peace. He pleaded for reconciliation and a halt to the violence.

Among the groups which carried the cross at different stages in the procession to the City Hall were church leaders, church women, people from Bhambayi, monitors from the Ecumenical Monitoring Programme in South Africa (Empsa) and youth leaders from the IFP, the ANC, the Azanian Peoples' Organisation (AZAPO), the Democratic Party (DP) and the National Party (NP).

After the flowering of the cross, the cross was handed to the people of Bhambayi by the Revd Dr Stanley Mogoba, as a reminder to the residents of the strife-torn township that peace and harmony are possible, even when people hold different political views.

As a tragic postscript to the Good Friday service, two days later on Easter Sunday, a woman kneeling to pray at the flowered cross set up in Bhambayi was shot as she prayed. Would peace never come?

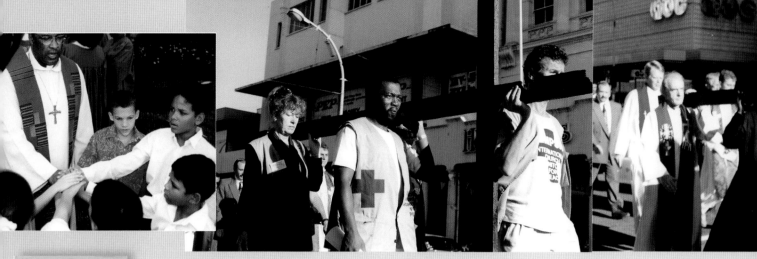

The Bhambayi Cross

This prayer depicts Bhambayi, one of the violence-ravaged places not far from the centre of the city of Durban. Bhambayi was, in fact, "Bombay", the name given by Mahatma Gandhi, who lived there during his stay in South Africa. The warring factions at Bhambayi were from the IFP and the ANC. In this period we were so engulfed with concern over the tension between these political groups that other issues of identity – such as relations between Indians and Africans – were eclipsed.

As I recited the poem at the Good Friday service, women from Bhambayi walked solemnly down the aisle at Emmanuel Cathedral in Durban where the service began, bearing pieces from their burnt-down houses, to make a cross at the altar. The cross was used to lead the procession through the streets of Durban. At the end of the second part of the service, it was ritually decorated with flowers. After the service the cross with its flowers was taken and placed in Bhambayi.

I wondered about words and poems, prayers and peace services, when I learned that on that Easter Sunday, a woman was shot while kneeling before that very cross.

Betty Govinden

The Bhambayi Cross

pieces of wood
broken and burnt
stained with blood of family
derelict in the smouldering heap
the smell of death
in dusty roads
sounds of weeping
darkness and gloom

my god, my god, why have you
    abandoned us
why have you forgotten us
forsaken us

pieces of wood
pierce the wounded side
lightning and thunder
shots of gunfire
rending cries of
mothers and daughters
in the sleepless houses
waiting for the first light

this is a cross
too heavy to bear

my god, my god, why have you
    abandoned us
why have you forgotten us
forsaken us

cry rage and revenge
slaughter and destruction
how long will this be
terror in the faces of children
hatred and fear

over a wilderness of shacks
the other side of the city wall
longing for peace

my god, my god, why have you
    abandoned us
why have you forgotten us
forsaken us

come
let us carry these pieces of wood
once part of the same ancient
    tree
used to build houses, proud and
    sturdy
now charred ruins of dwelling
    places
scattered and aloof

bind piece with piece
to build one cross

cross of bhambayi
shelter me
hide me from the
pain and agony
as the blood
like justice
flows from the cross

from the soil
sprouts a new year of freedom
    and healing
for captives
maimed in body and
maimed in hope

sacred mystery
on this holy ground
tree of redemption
the flowering tree which withers
and blossoms again
from eden to calvary
to easter...
in bhambayi...

The power of the cross

The first Good Friday service I participated in was in 1994, having moved to Durban from Port Elizabeth. The service started in Emmanuel Cathedral, and the cross was made from burnt timbers salvaged from the houses of an IFP member and an ANC member in Bhambayi informal settlement. The two pieces of timber were combined in the cross, as a symbol of the healing and reconciling power of the cross of Jesus Christ.

This was a few weeks prior to the historic 1994 elections which turned South Africa into a democracy in which all citizens were able to vote for the first time, and this heightened the symbolism of the cross.

I was part of the group which carried the cross out of the Cathedral onto the streets of the city, to the first change-over point. This made a deep impact on me in terms of the power of the cross, and the power of the witness of Diakonia over the years of its witness to the citizens of Durban.

I barely made it back to my congregation in Glenashley to start our 9am Good Friday service, where I explained where I had been, and spoke about the significance of the cross I had helped to carry. There were some visitors from the United Kingdom (UK) in the congregation that morning, who carried that story back home with them – and the witness spread.

Revd Ian Booth
Deputy Vice-Chair
Diakonia Council of Churches

Out of the flames of death, a cross of peace . . .

GOOD FRIDAY SERVICE
FOR PEACEFUL ELECTIONS
UKHETHO OLUNOKUTHULA

Emmanuel Cathedral, Durban
1 April 1994, 6.30 am
Sermon : Dr Beyers Naudé

WAR AND PEACE: BHAMBAYI residents carry a cross (top right) made of burnt beams from homes destroyed in their township strangled by violence, at yesterday's Good Friday peace procession when hundreds of Christians marched through the streets of Durban to the City Hall. Later the cross was presented to residents to erect in the strife-torn area as a symbol of peace (picture left). Flowers, placed by marchers on the cross on the steps of the city hall, were handed to Nomandhla Shandu, the daughter of slain Umlazi peace committee worker

Isaac Shandu. In the moving ceremony organised jointly by Diakonia and the Durban and District Council of Churches, Christians paid tribute to the thousands of victims of violence in Natal and prayed that elections in the province would be free, fair and peaceful.

Church leaders in the procession included Arch-bishop Dennis Hurley, Archbishop Wilfrid Napier, Bishop Ross Cuthbertson and Bishop Norman Hudson. Veteran ANC member Archie Gumede was also there.

Pictures: JOHN WOODROOF & SIMON du BUISSON

Blessed are the peacemakers · Babusisiwe abalamulayo

GOOD FRIDAY ECUMENICAL SERVICE

INKONZO YEPHASIKA YAMABANDLA AHLUKENE

Service at Emmanuel Cathedral
Inkonzo e-Emmanuel Cathedral
14 April 1995, 6.30am
Sermon: Rev Athol Jennings

"Blessed are the peacemakers, for they shall be called the children of God"
"Babusisiwe abalamulayo ngokuba bayobizwa ngabantwana bakaNkulunkulu"
Matthew 5:9

Organised by the Diakonia Council of Churches, PO Box 1879 Durban 4000 Phone (031) 305-6001 Fax (031) 305-2486

A MIRACULOUS TRANSFORMATION

The first non-racial election was due to be held three weeks after the 1994 Good Friday service. At the time of the service the IFP was still boycotting the election, in the context of ongoing political violence in the province.

An unprecedented campaign of public and private prayer and the significant intervention of an international mediator led to a breakthrough and the entrance of the IFP into the elections just days before 26 April 1994, resulting in a scramble on the part of the Independent Electoral Commission (IEC) to print new ballot papers and distribute them in time: some were still being printed on the second day of what proved to be a three-day election.

The consequence was what many have called a miraculous transformation of the political atmosphere in KwaZulu and Natal. The election period was extraordinarily peaceful despite the massive logistical problems on the election days, as well as on the days of counting, and despite the worst political violence this country has ever seen in the weeks before the elections.

Then we experienced the remarkable peace that prevailed during and immediately after the elections: the wonderful patience of lengthy queues waiting to vote; the unbelievable joy of those voting for the first time.

The deeply moving inauguration of President Nelson Mandela was a day of great pride and gratitude for all South Africans, followed by the opening of the country's first democratically elected parliament and the inauguration of a Government of National Unity. A wave of enthusiasm for reconciliation passed over the whole country. God's hand in all this was acknowledged by many.

After the elections, political violence dropped steadily. The threatened violent resistance by the white right wing failed to materialise. A remarkable degree of national unity was forged by President Mandela and Vice-Presidents Thabo Mbeki and F.W. de Klerk. Procedures and infrastructure for implementation of the Reconstruction and Development Programme (RDP) were set up, and the process of writing a new constitution got under way. People of all persuasions realised how blessed the country was to have a State President of the stature of Nelson Mandela.

And yet, looking back a year later, there was a sense that expectations had not been met, and promises made in the election campaign had not been delivered. Life for the poorest people had hardly changed.

KwaZulu-Natal got off to a very shaky start. Many considered the elections in this province to be much less than free and fair. The dispute about where the capital was to be situated was still unresolved. Tensions between IFP and ANC continued. King Goodwill Zwelithini's efforts to play a non-political role and become independent from the IFP added a new dimension to the power struggle.

Deaths in political violence in January 1995 reached the highest level for any month since April 1994. There was no certainty that people in rural KwaZulu-Natal would be allowed to vote in the November local government elections, or even to register, because traditional leaders insisted that international mediation take place, as had been agreed prior to the April 1994 elections.

THE DIAKONIA COUNCIL OF CHURCHES IS FORMED

Important changes had taken place in the ecumenical field over the year since the 1994 Good Friday service. The year had started with two agencies in Durban, the DDCC and Diakonia, working alongside one another and complementing each other, as they had done for many years. The year ended with one ecumenical organisation – the Diakonia Council of Churches, dedicated at a colourful ecumenical service on International Human Rights Day, 10 December 1994.

The process towards greater unity among the churches operating in the Durban area took a long time and was costly to both agencies, but the church was no doubt stronger because of this amalgamation.

The KwaZulu-Natal situation posed a great challenge for Durban churches. Fortunately, the new Diakonia Council of Churches, with a larger staff and more member churches, would be more able to face the challenges than either Diakonia or the DDCC.

HEAL, RECONCILE AND BUILD FOR PEACE

The theme of *'Heal, Reconcile and Build for Peace'* was to run behind all Diakonia's activities in 1995. There were many obstacles to achieving these ideals, as Bishop Gunnar Lislerud of Norway noted when he reported to church leaders in March on his visits to KwaZulu-Natal communities suffering from political violence, racism, unemployment and unequal access to land.

The tenth annual Good Friday service and procession was held on 14 April 1995. It drew a record number of participants and received messages of support from many people, including individuals and groups in Europe.

Act of Commitment

Make us willing, Lord,
    to share with all our fellow South Africans
    the gift of your peace.
Make us poor in spirit,
    make us gentle.
Teach us to hunger and thirst for what is right,
    to be merciful and pure in heart.
Show us how to be peacemakers.
And, if we are persecuted in the cause of right,
    help us to rejoice
    and be glad to suffer for the sake of your holy name.

Blessing

Let us go out into the world to be peacemakers
    wherever we live and work.
May we know peace in our own hearts
    and be at peace with God.
May peace reign in our families and communities
    in this city, province and country
    and throughout the world,
The peace that Jesus made
    through his death on the cross.
And may the blessing of God the Father,
    God the Son
    and God the Holy Spirit
        descend upon us and remain with us always.

The theme *'Blessed are the Peacemakers'* was an encouragement to many people to give themselves generously to the task of being peacemakers.

The service started at Emmanuel Cathedral, where the sermon was preached by the Revd Athol Jennings of the Vuleka Trust, who had been much involved in the peace process in KwaZulu-Natal. The procession through the streets of Durban concluded outside the Durban City Hall, where the ceremony of flowering the cross gave an opportunity for members of the congregation to express their commitment to be peacemakers.

Each person present was given a prayer card and a small cross with the service theme to take home, as a focus of prayer and a reminder of the commitments made on Good Friday.

Focus on Good Friday Service

This year's Good Friday Service, the tenth, attracted more than two thousand people to Emmanuel Cathedral, Durban for the annual event. The theme of the service was "Blessed are the Peacemakers."

The Service which started at 6:30 a.m. was followed by a procession through the streets of Durban and ended with the "flowering of the cross" at the steps of the Durban City Hall.

The following pictures tell the story.

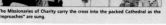

The Missionaries of Charity carry the cross into the packed Cathedral as the "reproaches" are sung.

Rev. Athol Jennings of Vuleka Trust, who preached on the theme "Blessed are the Peacemakers."

God performs a mighty work on Good Friday

Before my family and I came from Estcourt to Durban, our lives had just passed through three trying times and difficult tragedies:

(a) Our home, which was the mission house at Estcourt, was petrol-bombed in August 1992 while all our children and my wife Swazi were in the house. By God's grace they were all saved.

(b) Four months later my younger brother, Musa, died in a mysterious way that we could not understand.

(c) On 19 December 1992 my wife, who was driving, and three children who were passengers were all in a car that was behind me in a convoy which was involved in an accident. They were all in that accident, and my daughter Lungile did not make it: she died. My wife's legs were both broken. This accident left me devastated, broken and confused.

After two days the doctors in Ladysmith called me and asked me to sign a consent for Swazi, my wife, to have both legs amputated. I could not even want to think of that idea. I had a very strong conviction that my wife will walk again. For me, to amputate Swazi was to close the door for God to perform His miracle of love. The only thing I wanted was to open the door for God to show us His loving kindness. Amputating her, for me, was to close that door.

Unfortunately I could not wait for Swazi to wake up from a coma so that we could together make a collective decision. My opinion was different from that of all the professional doctors: to amputate her, for me, was to kill her fighting spirit. I could not see her fighting for life after she had been amputated.

Three months later I asked for Swazi to be transferred to Addington Hospital, which was closer to me and with doctors I could trust and who understood my belief.

On the big day, Good Friday 1995, God heard my prayer. The Good Friday service and procession was to begin from the Roman Catholic Cathedral and then process to the City Hall.

I drove my car and stopped in the street and asked my wife to drive herself to the City Hall. That would be the first time she would drive since her accident in December 1992.

I now can testify that from that day Swazi began to live a different life. She could drive and walk with the aid of crutches. Today the person of whom it was said that she will never walk again, she is now walking and driving.

I can testify that on that Good Friday God performed a mighty work for me, my wife Swazi and my family. It was on that Good Friday that God affirmed His love for me and my family. Today I can say with boldness that I confirm that God loves me. The sad thing is that I do not love Him as I ought.

"I will praise you, O Lord my God, with all my heart: I will glorify your name for ever" Psalm 86:12

Bishop Elijah Thwala

ABEFUNDISI beDiakonia Council of Churches, eThekwini bazobe besibambe ngaloluhlobo isiphambano njengophawu lokuqanyulezwa kukaJesu Krestu enkozweni yePhasika esiqubulo sayo esizobe sithi "Babusisiwe Abadalu uxolo." Izokuba se-St. Emannuel Cathedral kulelidolobha kusukela ngolwesiHlanu mhlaka April 14 ngo-6.30 ekuseni. Ababo bakala esithombeni kusukela kwesokunxele nguMfu. Freddy Mayekiso, Arch. Bishop Dennis Hurley, uMfu. Sam Khumalo noBishop. Phillip Russell. (ISITHOMBE NGU-ABE PHUNGULA).

Inkonzo Yephasika
Good Friday Service

**Isiphambano
Sokuphila**

**The Cross
of Life**

Durban City Hall · 5 April 1996, 6.30 am

THE CONTEXT

Diakonia's area of operation is what was called the Durban Functional Region, extending from the Tugela River in the north to the Umkomaas River in the south and to Cato Ridge in the west. Just under four million people – that is, half the population of KwaZulu-Natal – were estimated to live in this region in 1995.

In an area beset with socio-economic-political problems, most poor people had seen no change in their living conditions since the national elections of 1994. The province was preparing for delayed local government elections, now planned for May 1996. These preparations brought to those in greatest need not only the promise of basic services but also the threat of increased violence. Unemployment, inequality, crime and the high prevalence of HIV/AIDS were the backdrop to the context in which Diakonia was working.

There was an urgent need to establish political and economic stability if any efforts towards peace, reconciliation and development were to succeed.

HEAL, RECONCILE AND BUILD FOR PEACE

It was helpful to have this unifying theme for the work of all the programmes in the organisation, as they sought to encourage and enable the churches in the geographic area to deal with the problems of their context.

In spite of work to help people understand and accept the dynamics of democracy, political violence surged, with several massacres in the lower South Coast area in the days before Christmas 1995. On Christmas Day a massacre at Shobashobane claimed 19 lives and drove many more from their homes. At the beginning of January 1996 a pastoral visit by church leaders to the area was organised.

Responding to fears of heightened tension and violence around the local government elections due on 19 May 1996, the Ecumenical Peacemakers' Programme (EPP) was set up by the KwaZulu-Natal Church Leaders' Group (KZNCLG). This provided for trained local and international peacemakers to monitor political rallies and other events, and to intervene as mediators.

THE CROSS OF LIFE

The crowd that gathered for the eleventh ecumenical Good Friday service on 5 April 1996 was so large that, although the service took place for the first time inside the City Hall, the largest venue used to that date, for several hundred people there was standing room only.

The theme *'The Cross of Life'* was beautifully portrayed by a tree carved by artist Dina Cormick, which provided the focus of the service, procession and flowering ceremony. Many commented on the powerful impact of the spotlit cross procession through the darkened hall as Evelyn Bartsch sang the spiritual *'Calvary'* with great feeling.

After readings, prayers and singing, the Anglican Bishop of Natal, Bishop Rubin Phillip, preached and then led the procession out into the streets, to process right around the City Hall, to its main entrance steps on the city square, in a gesture of prayer for the city leaders and all those who would be elected at the local level within the next few weeks.

After the flowering of the cross and the conclusion of the service on the steps of the City Hall, the cross was taken to Methodist Central City Mission, where it remained as the focus of an ongoing prayer vigil.

This annual service by now had become a significant way of symbolising the work of the Diakonia Council of Churches to help to transform the conditions of suffering people.

GOOD FRIDAY: The Diakonia Council of Churches will again hold a Good Friday Ecumenical service which will involve the carrying of a cross through Durban streets. Artist Dina Cormick is seen sculpting the tree which will be used as a cross on the day.

PICTURE: PATRICK MTOLO

Prayers for election peace

MERCURY REPORTER

THE Diakonia Council of Churches will use this year's Good Friday Ecumenical service to pray for peaceful local government elections on May 29

Diakonia director Paddy Kearney said yesterday this year's theme would be "The Cross of Life".

The Good Friday service will mark the beginning of 50 days of prayer in homes and churches culminating in the March for Jesus on May 25, the eve of the Pentecost, a few days before the elections.

The service will begin inside Durban's city hall at 6.30pm on Friday April 5.

The service will entail a procession which will involve the carrying of a cross through city streets.

Mr Kearney said all who attended would be given a prayer card.

Act of Faith and Commitment

> Choose life that you may be
> a leaven for the human family.
> Then shall you live in peace
> as justice bears the fruit of freedom throughout all the world.

Because of our belief in Jesus as redeemer,
we choose to be a people who uproot the sources of violence and oppression
within ourselves and within our society.
Because of our belief in Jesus as redeemer,
we choose to commit ourselves to change our lives
so that others may have life in abundance.

> Choose life that you may be
> a leaven for the human family.
> Then shall you live in peace
> as justice bears the fruit of freedom throughout all the world.

Because of our belief in the church as community,
we choose to be a community that dances and sings
in spite of the tendency of our times to despair and cynicism.
Because of our belief in the church as community,
we commit ourselves to faithfulness to God,
to one another and to the whole human family.

> Choose life that you may be
> a leaven for the human family.
> Then shall you live in peace
> as justice bears the fruit of freedom throughout all the world.

Prayer for the elections

God of justice, righteousness and peace,
    we long to overcome the pain and division of KwaZulu-Natal
    and all the violence that ravages our communities.
We long for a democracy
    that ensures opportunity for all to seek life in all its fullness.
Bless our elections:
    help us to ensure that they are free, fair and peaceful.
May your Holy Spirit inspire all to vote responsibly
    and with concern for the whole community.
May candidates and political parties
    act with integrity and restraint.
Guide all election officials, all media workers, all who provide security,
    that they may act with fairness and impartiality.
Help all monitors and observers,
    all who participate in the Churches' Democracy Campaign,
    and the Ecumenical Peacemakers' Programme
      to carry out their tasks with wisdom and courage.
May all our people accept the election results
    in the spirit of true democracy.
May those who are elected carry out their duties with justice and
      compassion,
    sensitive to the needs of all.
May they encourage a spirit of reconciliation and unity,
    and draw our people to participate in local government.
All this we ask through Jesus Christ our Lord.

Inkonzo Yephasika Good Friday Service

Isiphambano Sokuphila — The Cross of Life

Durban City Hall · 5 April 1996, 6.30 am

uJesu umPhilisi olimeleyo
Jesus THE WOUNDED HEALER

**GOOD FRIDAY SERVICE ◆ INKONZO YEPHASIKA
PREACHER ◆ FR. MICHAEL LAPSLEY
28 MARCH 1997 ◆ 6:15 AM
DURBAN CITY HALL**

SIGNS OF HOPE AND PROMISES OF HARD WORK

The prayers, pledges and campaigns for peace in the province seemed finally to bear some fruit in the year since the 1996 Good Friday service. The number of people losing their lives in political violence was still unacceptable, at around 40 each month, but reflected a positive trend compared to the monthly death toll of 70 during 1995. While much still needed to be done to ensure that the fragile political peace endured, there was at last some space to focus on the massive task of development in one of the country's poorest provinces.

The new National Constitution, accepted by all parties, had taken legal effect, and the task of making all citizens aware of the rights guaranteed thereby was under way.

In KwaZulu-Natal, the repeated postponement of the local elections, due to political conflict and administrative problems, worsened the climate of instability and confusion. The killing of more than a dozen prospective election candidates undermined both the election process and peace efforts.

Then, in May, came an attack on women of the Zulu royal family in KwaMashu. The mob attack, sparked by the invitation to ANC as well as IFP dignitaries to a function in an IFP-dominated area, resulted in the murder of Princess Nonhlanhla Zulu and the brutal injury of Queen Buhle and Princess Sibusile. Calls for restraint by political leaders and the arrest of several suspects helped to prevent a further round of violence.

Project Ukuthula, a peace initiative driven by the churches and supported by the political leaders, contributed to efforts to create a climate for free, fair and peaceful elections.

The local elections finally took place in June 1996. Widespread acceptance of the results was a significant factor in the reduction of violence after voting day.

PARTNERSHIP IN GOD'S WORK OF TRANSFORMATION

Diakonia Council of Churches, in keeping with the 1996 theme, focussed its attention on equipping the churches, as part of civil society, to be actively involved in issues troubling the province. These included unemployment, disrupted schooling and inadequate education, crime and the restructuring of the South African Police Service (SAPS). Ongoing violence, particularly rape and other abuse against women and children, and the failures of the justice system also became focal issues for the churches.

An interfaith service was held in the City Hall prior to the first provincial hearings of the Truth & Reconciliation Commission (TRC) in May 1996, at the TRC's request. The organisation helped to organise peace services at the request of local government, in thanksgiving after the local government elections and again at the beginning of December to pray that there would not be a resurgence of the violence experienced the previous Christmas. These, in addition to the annual Good Friday service, gave opportunities to share a model of creative liturgy, linking faith with the pressing current social issues in the area.

JESUS THE WOUNDED HEALER

By this time the annual ecumenical Good Friday service had become Diakonia's largest and most important public event. The enormous amount of work and preparation required was justified because this service symbolised and summarised all the activities of the Diakonia Council of Churches.

So much of the organisation's work had been with suffering people. The Good Friday services have always given an opportunity to reflect on the significance of suffering in the light of Jesus' passion and death.

Through the efforts on four priority issues: peace, democracy, economic empowerment and justice, as well as HIV/AIDS, Diakonia was working alongside the churches to help people in the Durban Functional Region realise that victory over the forces of sin and death was within their grasp, through Jesus' victory.

In 1997 the theme for the Good Friday service was *'Jesus the Wounded Healer'*. It was a privilege to have Fr Michael Lapsley SSM as preacher, whose very presence gave striking expression to that theme. As one who bears in his own body the marks of violence from a parcel bomb explosion in Harare, he was able to empathise with and understand those who had suffered from various forms of violence, especially the political violence that plagued KwaZulu-Natal for so long.

The 1997 service began in the City Hall, where there was standing room only. Highlights were the sermon by Fr Lapsley, the spotlit procession with the cross, and the dance by the Siwela Sonke Dance Theatre. From the City Hall the congregation walked in silent procession around the block, ending outside the front entrance with the flowering of the cross. Church leaders gave a healing blessing to many surviviors of violence.

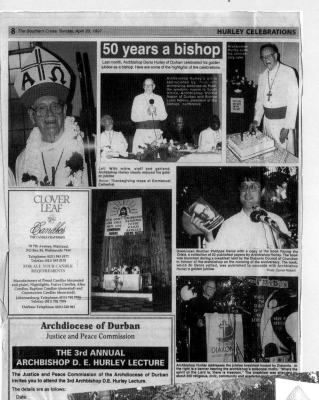

ARCHBISHOP HURLEY'S GOLDEN JUBILEE

On 19 March 1997, ten days before the Good Friday service, Archbishop Denis Hurley OMI celebrated the 50th anniversary of his ordination as bishop. As he had founded Diakonia in 1976 and was a Patron Emeritus of the Diakonia Council of Chuches, the occasion was marked by a special Golden Jubilee Breakfast.

The Breakfast was a splendid event, with 250 guests including Premier Dr Frank Mdlalose, Metro Mayor Obed Mlaba, Judge Ray Leon, and many heads of churches and leaders of other faiths. A trumpet flourish greeted the jubilarian as he entered the venue, and the choir of Natal University (now University of KwaZulu-Natal) sang: at the time the Archbishop was Chancellor of the University.

All the guests signed a large card depicting a gold mitre with highlights from the Archbishop's life, and a special message from President Nelson Mandela was read. The Archbishop was himself the guest speaker on the topic *'Memories of 50 years: from Segregation through Apartheid to Liberation and Democracy.'*

1997

Becoming a wounded healer

Extract from sermon by Father Michael Lapsley SSM

I greet you as one called myself to be a wounded healer.

Twenty four years ago my journey began in the City of Durban. When it began in 1973, I had two hands, two eyes: I could see clearly and hear clearly. I was expelled after three-and-a-half years and lived with our people in exile for 16 years – with people who, when they remembered Zion, wept. Then, in exile in Harare, I received an envelope with two religious magazines, one in English and one in Afrikaans. I opened the English one, and that detonated the bomb.

With the bomb, I was first the focus of evil. But then, of all that is good in humanity. I was enabled to make the bombing redemptive: to bring good out of evil. God helped me realise that if I was filled with hate and bitterness I would be a permanent victim. They would have failed to kill the body, but they would have killed the soul.

In that bomb I lost a great deal, but I gained a great deal also, and I am a better human being because of what happened to me. I am no longer just a survivor. I am a victor over hatred and death. I stand here to remind us of what it is we have done to one another. But also to remind us that the forces of love and compassion are stronger than the forces of hatred and death.

The same choice confronts everyone in South Africa, especially in KwaZulu-Natal. Who knows Good Friday better than the people of this province? Who knows better what it is to be crucified and to crucify others?

Many people in this province have every good reason to be full of hatred. But where will that lead? We will then be like the people of Bosnia. Or we can respond with the weapons of the gospel: we can take good out of evil and life out of death. We can choose whether we want to live as free people.

But to do that we have to admit to ourselves and one another that we do feel anger and bitterness, and we must create space for these stories. But in the end these must be left at the foot of the cross. Forgiveness is painful and costly. And we need God's help to do it.

Today as we go into the streets to say *'No'* to violence, it reminds us that we need to relate the stories of trauma and pain. Our Lord's story is one of pain and betrayal and sacrifice and crucifixion and death. But also of the signs of resurrection and new life.

My prayer for the people of KwaZulu-Natal is that today will be a turning point in the very long journey of hatred and death towards compassion and new life.

After the resurrection, Jesus appeared to the disciples, but Thomas was not there. He said he would not believe unless he saw the wounds and put his fingers in them. Then the risen Christ appeared to Thomas, and he believed.

While the marks of your crucifixion will remain for ever, let us move from the death of Good Friday to the life of the resurrection. Let us become wounded healers.

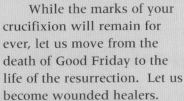

Jesus
the Wounded Healer

'That which was a stitch of pain, has become the path to the priesthood.'
Lembu Jang Inc. Kongti society 1910

UJesu uMphilisi OLimelzwe   Jesus the Wounded Healer

GOOD FRIDAY SERVICE • INKONZO YEPHASIKA
PREACHER • FR. MICHAEL LAPSLEY
28 MARCH 1997 • 6:15 AM
DURBAN CITY HALL

GOOD FRIDAY SERVICE
INKONZO YEPHASIKA

UKUPHILA NGEGAZI LIKA JESU · · LIFE THROUGH JESUS' BLOOD ·

10 April 1998 – 6.15am

ICC – International Convention Centre
45 Ordnance Road · Durban

Address: Bishop Mvume Dandala

Organised by the Diakonia Council of Churches · Ecumenical Centre · 20 St Andrew's Street · Durban 4001 · Tel. (031) 305-6001 · Fax (031) 305-2486

Designed and produced by GRAPHICOS

NEW RIGHTS, NEW RESPONSIBILITIES

The year since Good Friday 1997 was one of continuing challenges for everyone working for peace, democracy, economic justice and social transformation in the region.

Having succeeded in electing new local government representatives in 1996, KwaZulu-Natal had rolled up its sleeves and begun living and working with the rights enshrined in South Africa's new constitution. But the development constraints in the Durban Functional Region, which included both extremely affluent white residential areas and very poor townships, informal settlements and surrounding rural areas, were enormous. The new rights would be accompanied by new responsibilities to assist in socio-economic and political transformation in the region.

In spite of the Human Rights Committee recording a 31.7% drop from 1996 in the total of deaths as a result of political violence, with the figure of politically related deaths in Durban in 1997 reaching 89, pockets of violence continued to exist, most notably in Richmond in the Natal Midlands and in Umlazi's H-Section. It was feared that, if the violence in these areas was any indicator, fighting for political turf might throw the province back into turmoil in the run-up to the 1999 general elections. This would mean that the churches' role in reconciliation in general, and in conflict mediation in particular, would be crucial in the coming year.

PARTNERS IN FAITH AND ACTION

The mandate of the Diakonia Council of Churches was – and continues to be – to serve the Durban Functional Region, an area which represents a microcosm of the world and which posed, and continues to pose, great challenges to design programmes that serve the disparate conditions under which its people live. In order to bridge these gaps, the organisation enables people from all walks of life to reach out to each other, to share ideas and resources.

Diakonia works in partnership with the churches – through the leadership of both the mainline and independent churches. Its aim is to inform, motivate, support and influence leaders in the churches who can in turn reach out to many more who can contribute to peace, development and a better quality of life for the four million people in this region.

All the organisation's work and life and ethos was summarised in 1997 into an organisational theme for the year, which subsequently became a continuing backdrop for the years to come: 'Partners in Faith and Action.'

LIFE THROUGH JESUS' BLOOD

It was from the field of health that the 1998 Good Friday service's theme was taken, to draw attention to the immense suffering caused by the AIDS pandemic. It was estimated that this pandemic had already claimed the lives of 150 000 people in KwaZulu-Natal between 1991 and 1997 – 50 000 of them having died in 1997 alone.

The intensity of the involvement of the Diakonia Council of Churches in the AIDS issue had increased during the year. The Good Friday service provided a way of linking this terrible suffering directly with the suffering of Christ, and providing theological and spiritual resources as well as strength to the churches, as they intensified their commitment, put into words in this act of worship in the theme 'Life through Jesus' Blood.'

The service was held in the International Convention Centre because of the growing numbers attending. It brought thousands of people from across the political and religious spectrum together to pledge themselves to the struggle against HIV/AIDS.

The sermon was preached by Presiding Bishop Mvume Dandala of the Methodist Church, and the Siwela Sonke Dance Theatre performed a dance depicting the theme. A litany of healing was shared. Then the thousands of people in the congregation solemnly walked through the streets of Durban, silently mourning the death of those who had died from AIDS-related diseases, and drawing attention to the needs of those living with the disease.

At the City Hall steps, people decorated the cross with a 'red ribbon' of anthiriums and carnations, as a sign of their commitment to prevent the spread of AIDS and to care for all people affected by AIDS.

People were invited to pin onto the cross the photos and names of people who had died of AIDS-related diseases.

Everyone received a button with the theme of the service as well as a prayer card with ideas to help people become involved in AIDS ministry and a list of resource organisations with contact details. Following the service, many people from congregations all over Durban contacted Diakonia's AIDS Programme about starting a ministry to people affected by HIV/AIDS.

The cross was taken to McCord Hospital after the service, where it remained for all to see the solidarity of the churches in Durban.

ANG NEWS MAY/JUNE 1940

ABOVE: AIDS was the theme of this year's Good Friday service in Durban held by the Diakonia Council of Churches. Seen at the service placing red flowers on a cross in the memory of those who died or suffer from AIDS were from left to right: former KwaZulu-Natal premier Dr Frank Mdlalose, premier Dr Ben Ngubane, the KZN minister of health, Dr Zweli Mkhize (at the back), the minister of home affairs, Dr Mangosuthu Buthelezi and in front the minister of health Dr Nkosazana Zuma, watched by a member of the crowd.

Picture by Shelley Kjonstad

GOOD FRIDAY SERVICE
INKONZO YEPHASIKA

UKUPHILA NGEGAZI LIKA JESU
· LIFE THROUGH JESUS' BLOOD ·

10 April 1998 - 6.15am
ICC - International Convention Centre
45 Ordnance Road · Durban
Address: Bishop Mbawe Dandala

UKUPHILA NGEGAZI LIKA JESU
· LIFE THROUGH JESUS' BLOOD ·

1998

A humbling spiritual experience

The public witness I experienced from the very first Diakonia Good Friday service that I attended was a very humbling spiritual experience that I find difficult to put into words.

The carefully considered themes over the years have been very meaningful, and made me more conscious of the gospel teachings and Christ's sufferings for us and for those people who are still suffering for various reasons, such as poverty, HIV/AIDS, etc.

As Christians of different denominations, walking through the streets of Durban in silent procession as one in the body of Christ is something I will always treasure.

I was also blessed to be part of the initial arrangements around the flowering of the cross. Being part of the preparation and flowering of the cross, which emphasises the hope and triumph of the resurrection over the suffering of the cross, was one of the highlights of the service for me.

Daphne Goad

Enacted theology

Vulnerable people are continually being crucified by the powers of the world. God is continually self-emptying, suffering with the most suffering.

The Good Friday services express this in an enacted theology that draws an enormous response from people at the margins of society, repressed and oppressed.

They respond because they recognise God at work alongside those whom the powerful despise and reject – as Jesus was despised and rejected.

Testimony of a person who is HIV-positive

"I was diagnosed HIV-positive in 1994. Since then I have experienced much rejection, including from my own church. People there felt I was dirty, filthy in the eyes of God. But my family has stood by me. And Jesus has been my best friend. He is the best thing that ever happened to me."

> **Musa Njoko**
> National Association of
> People Living with HIV/AIDS
> (NAPWA)

Commitment

Lord Jesus Christ,
as we remember your passion and death,
help us to accept the challenge of AIDS:
 to protect the healthy and calm
  the fearful;
 to offer courage to those in pain;
 to embrace the dying;
 to care for their orphans
  and families;
 to console the bereaved;
 to support all those who care.

We offer our energies,
 our imaginations
 and our commitment.

Unite us in your love
 and free us from fear of this
  disease.

We trust in the resurrection to come
 that you may be glorified
 now and for ever.

uJesu iThemba Lakusasa + Jesus our Hope for the Future

GOOD FRIDAY SERVICE • INKONZO YEPHASIKA

2 APRIL 1999 • 6:15 AM

DURBAN CITY HALL

DIAKONIA COUNCIL OF CHURCHES, 1st floor, Ecumenical Centre, 20 St Andrew's Street, Durban, 4001. P.O. Box 61341, Bishopsgate 4008. E-mail: diak@iafrica.com Tel: (031) 305-6001 Fax: (031) 305-2486

Amanda Dillon

THE LONG ROAD TO DEVELOPMENT

The TRC was an important response to the challenge to overcome South Africa's terrible past and build a united nation. Its findings were presented in October 1998. It served at least to throw some light on the hidden histories of South Africa and to illuminate the need and the possibility for reconciliation between those who endured and those who committed human rights violations. The publication of its report marked not only a closure but a point at which all South Africans needed to take over responsibility for the long process of hearing and healing each other.

South Africa's first post-apartheid census results were released in October 1998. They gave a statistical measure of the extreme disparities between rich and poor – a gap that was wider than anywhere in the world, except Brazil.

As poor people in the Durban area felt the brunt of globalisation of the economy, they also felt the need for globalisation of compassion and justice. The Peace to the City initiative of the World Council of Churches (WCC) was one model of how those who are not in positions of power and wealth can link together to 'globalise' their experience of overcoming conflict and distrust. Stories of efforts to build peace in Durban, along with stories from six other world cities, were shared with people from all over the world at the Peace to the City assembly in Harare.

The peace in KwaZulu-Natal was a fragile one, shattered sporadically by multiple killings, caused by both political and personal feuds. The need for leadership in building caring and secure communities became more apparent than ever.

Reports of horrific rapes highlighted the continued vulnerability of South Africans, and especially women and children, to human rights violations. 1998 marked the 50th anniversary of the United Nations Universal Declaration of Human Rights. It also marked South Africa becoming the country with the highest rate of rape and the second highest rate of murder in the world.

A TIME FOR ORGANISING

As the country prepared for the second democratic election, it was clear that this time there would be sheer hard work rather than the emotional tidal wave that carried the country through the first. Democracy education was not so much about informing people how to vote but why it was important that they vote. As the political parties began their election campaigns, it became clear that the central theme would be delivery. There was certainly progress to be reported on many fronts: water and electrification, wider access to welfare grants, progressive new labour relations legislation. At the same time, levels of corruption were unacceptable and threatened the ability of any party to deliver effective services to the millions who needed them.

The churches and communities with whom Diakonia Council of Churches was working had been actively addressing all the burning issues – economic justice, peace and violence, democracy, and HIV/AIDS – during the year. As the time came to plan the Good Friday service, it became clear that a widely-encompassing theme was necessary.

JESUS OUR HOPE FOR THE FUTURE

The main focus of the service on 2 April 1999, with its theme *'Jesus our Hope for the Future'*, was on praying for strength to tackle the problems of poverty, health, crime, violence and political intolerance with new hope for the new millennium.

The service started at the City Hall with meditative singing. A large burnt wooden cross was carried slowly into the darkened hall through the congregation, accompanied by the Siwela Sonke Dance Theatre, drum and horn. It was placed on the stage as the backdrop for the prayers, singing and challenging sermon preached by the Revd Charity Majiza, General Secretary of the SACC.

People who could not get in to the packed hall waited outside to join the solemn silent procession as it made its way around the City Hall to the steps at the front. As the three thousand people processed to the solemn tolling of one bell of St Paul's Anglican Church nearby, they recalled the death of Jesus and mourned all those who had died as a result of crime, violence and HIV/AIDS.

Flowers were placed by members of the congregation on a shape of Africa fixed to the cross, as a sign of their commitment to participate in the transformation of society. The cross was lifted up to the joy of the people, as they sang and then prayed their commitment in the new hope given by the resurrection.

METRO Mayor Obed Mlaba and Bishop Rubin Phillip, of the Diakonia Council of Churches, unveil Durban's peace bus, with the enthusiastic support of passengers from the city's various peace initiatives

Mynah bus spreads message of peace

DAILY NEWS REPORTER

THE message of peace will be rumbling through the streets of Durban after a colourful Mynah "peace bus" was unveiled in the city yesterday.

The aim is to promote peace in the run-up to next year's elections while the bus zips along its daily routes through the city.

The brightly decorated bus is the idea of the Durban Peace to the City Campaign, spearheaded by Diakonia Council of Churches. It forms part of a global programme called "Peace to the City Campaign," aimed at promoting peace worldwide.

Durban is the seventh city internationally to join the campaign.

Bishop Rubin Phillip of Diakonia said the initiative started in Johannesburg when a church leader called on ecumenical leaders to become involved in peace campaigns. It was adopted by the World Council of Churches, which identified a number of cities around the world to spearhead such a project.

"The initiative is set to address all kinds of violence. We would also like to encourage individuals, communities and every politician to work for the promotion of peace," he said.

The Rev Mike Vorster, coordinator of the Durban campaign, said the Mynah bus was an ideal way of sending a message of peace to thousands of people.

He said they were looking at other ways of spreading the message to other areas.

The peace initiative also received the blessing of metro mayor Obed Mlaba, who described it as a vision to "work towards a sustainable peaceful city" and to "make Durban an island of peace".

Earlier this week the mayor lambasted fellow councillors, accusing them of stalling well-advanced plans to merge the metro's anti-crime efforts.

❑ For more information the peace bus, visit the we www.durbanpeace.org.za

The seed of hope

When I started to work for Diakonia Council of Churches in January 2000, I noticed that my predecessor, Makhosi Nzimande, had left in her desk drawer a copy of the 1999 Good Friday service booklet. At the back of the booklet I noticed that there was a small packet containing a few seeds, which people were invited to take home and plant after the service as an expression of hope. I was interested in the description given of the seeds as those of an *Acacia Natalitia* tree, a strain of *Acacia Karoo*. I kept the packet in a safe place.

A while later a work colleague of my mine, Alison Goldstone, showed me a picture of how well the trees had grown from the same seeds she had planted on her in-laws' property at Ifafa on the South Coast. This prompted me to plant the seeds which I still had. I waited until Freedom Day, 27 April 2004, to mark ten years of democracy. One of the seeds grew well. As we had a small garden I kept it in a container where it continued to grow.

When I was appointed rector of St John the Baptist Anglican Church, Pinetown, we moved into the rectory in Padfield Park. I decided to plant out the small tree into the grounds of the rectory. I did this on Arbour Day 2006. It grew well there.

Just before Good Friday this year (2008) I decided to replant the tree in the grounds of the church next to the newly established vegetable garden. I thought it would get more sun there and have more space to grow, as well as be appreciated by the church community. After a nearly ten year journey it has finally found a permanent home where it can flourish. New green leaves have appeared after the spring rains.

Revd Dr Andrew Warmback

Litany

When we are overcome by helplessness
    and feel we can never conquer crime and violence,
help us to remember:
Jesus, by your cross you have conquered sin and death.
    You are our hope for the future.

When the gap between rich and poor becomes ever wider
    and we feel that economic justice is an impossible dream,
help us to remember:
Jesus, by your cross you have conquered sin and death.
    You are our hope for the future.

When the barriers between Christians seem insurmountable
    and those between the world's great faiths lead to conflict and war,
help us to remember:
Jesus, by your cross you have conquered sin and death.
    You are our hope for the future.

Commitment

Lord Jesus Christ
you have saved us and given us new hope
    through your suffering, death and resurrection.
In our service today we have taken a cross of burnt wood
    and made it blossom with beauty and new life.
We commit ourselves
    to work for a similar transformation in our society.
We commit ourselves to be
    – people who live victoriously
    – people who are united in action for change
    – people who make a difference.
Help us to transform even the bleakest situations of
    crime
    violence
    poverty
    HIV/AIDS
    racism
    and despair
with the new hope you give us.

                                    Amen

A billion people are slaves to Third World debt.

Christian Aid
We believe in life before death

JUBILEE 2000 [SA]
KWAZULU NATAL

Seeds of new era

Warren Kandasamy, Melissa Moodley and Shaylen Padayachee with 10 000 seeds of the Acicia Karoo tree which will be packeted and distributed at the Diakonia Council of Churches' Good Friday service to be held at the Durban City Hall. The seeds signify the growth of our nation into the new millennium

Inkonzo Yephasika

Sibethelwe Ngobuphofu

Good Friday Service
21 April 2000 · 6.15am
ICC Convention Centre

Organised by the Diakonia Council of Churches
20 St. Andrews Street, Durban 4001
PO Box 61341, Bishopsgate 4008 · Phone: (031) 305-6001
Fax: (031) 305-2486 · E-mail: diak@iafrica.com

INTO THE NEW MILLENNIUM

Two months after the 1999 Good Friday service, on 2 June, South Africans went to the polls for the country's second democratic elections. While there had been some trepidation beforehand – especially in KwaZulu-Natal where political intolerance still reared its ugly head – the national elections were conducted in a remarkably peaceful and efficient manner.

In some senses, this was a sign that South Africa's transition to democracy was complete. The primary question facing the government was how to bridge the chasms dividing the population.

While no longer on the statute books, racial discrimination was still alive and well in the new South Africa. Economic differentiation lay at the heart of racial privilege. And the poverty continued for the great majority of the population.

While political conflict was greatly reduced, there was a disturbingly high incidence of criminal and domestic violence – the result, perhaps, of a population which had been extensively traumatised and destablised by political violence and apartheid. KwaZulu-Natal had the highest rate of HIV infection in the country and the fastest rate of infection in the world. HIV/AIDS was strongly linked with poverty. And service provision in KwaZulu-Natal was clearly lagging behind other provinces.

In spite of acknowledged progress by the democratic government, severe challenges remained.

VISIT OF INTERNATIONAL THEOLOGIANS

The Diakonia Council of Churches had the privilege of hosting two international theologians in 2000. The Revd Dr Philip Potter, former General Secretary of the WCC, visited Durban from 20 April to 9 May. His wife, the Revd Dr, subsequently Bishop Bärbel Wartenberg-Potter, at the time General Secretary of the German Council of Churches, was in Durban for a shorter period. Philip Potter had been invited to preach at the Good Friday service on the theme *'Crucified by Poverty'* and to give a number of addresses on economic justice in connection with Employment Sunday on 7 May.

It was a great joy that Bärbel was able to accompany him, and that she agreed to address various groups on feminist theology and the role of women in the church. Diakonia was grateful for their stimulating messages and gracious presence among us. The visits greatly strengthened the theological underpinning of Diakonia's work.

CRUCIFIED BY POVERTY

The Jubilee 2000 Good Friday service focussed on the ways in which poverty is a heavy cross which the majority of people in our country – and around the world – are forced to carry.

As the City Hall could no longer accommodate the large number of people who regularly attended, the service started at the International Convention Centre. More than three thousand people attended this, the fifteenth ecumenical Good Friday service in Durban.

Dancers from the Suria-Langa Dance Company provided a dramatic entrance to the service as they danced with incense to prepare the way for the cross. After readings, songs and a moving presentation of slides of specially commissioned photographs by Paul Weinberg – *'Faces of Poverty: Durban 2000'* – the sermon was delivered by the Revd Dr Philip Potter.

During the procession through the streets to the front of the City Hall, the cross was passed from the back of the procession to the front, over the heads of the silently walking congregation. All had the opportunity to carry the cross for a few moments, instead of only a small number of selected people: everyone found this a moving and joyful privilege.

The cross for the 2000 service was made by young people from the Evangelical Lutheran Church in Clermont, and from the Fine Arts Department at the University of Durban-Westville (now UKZN). It was made from "throw-away" materials, as a symbol of poverty. At the end of the service, the cross was taken to the Evangelical Lutheran Church, Clermont, and used for their Good Friday and Easter services.

People before money

Extract from sermon by the Revd Dr Philip Potter

We should never forget that Jesus declared about himself: *'The Son of Man came, not to be served, but to serve and to give his life as a ransom for many.'* He lived and moved among the simple, poor and despised people. He went about doing good – speaking and listening to people, healing the sick, comforting the sad and distressed. At the end, he was crucified precisely by the sort of people and systems that crucify so many people today in Durban, South Africa, Africa and the rest of the world.

Mark chapter 14, verses 1 to 11 tells us of Jesus' betrayal and crucifixion. But the emphasis is on the loving action of a woman who boldly came up to Jesus in the house of a man called Simon. She brought out a jar of very precious and expensive ointment. She poured all of it on his head. It was the act of a person who was expressing her gratitude for all that Jesus had given her – a new life and a new way of relating to others. She wanted to show in action her new understanding of life – not taking, grabbing, hiding, banking or investing, but giving.

The story ends with Judas seeking to betray Jesus. He was even offered money for this act. This is not strange for those of us who live in this country. We know what happened over three hundred years of history and what is going on now. Money comes before people and instead of people. That is why so many people are crucified by poverty.

Let us arise with Christ, our living Lord, and do to one another what this woman did to Christ, in attitude, word and deed.

Church vows to fight poverty

VERNON MCHUNU

THE church is determined to become the main player in the fight against poverty, and it hopes to prove this on Good Friday when scores of theologians call for communities to help eradicate poverty.

This was said yesterday by two church leaders, Anglican Bishop of Natal Rubin Phillip and Methodist Minister Carol Walsh.

They said that "Crucified by Poverty" would be the theme for this year's Good Friday service, as the church would begin to assume the role of attempting to bring about welfare and justice for every person.

The Rev Walsh said modern society was expected to take full responsibility for the suffering inflicted on so many people by poverty – highlighting findings of the Poverty and Inequality Report of 1998 that almost 20% of South Africans surviving below the poverty line lived in KwaZulu-Natal, making the province the country's second poorest after the Northern Province.

She appealed to employers to help eradicate poverty by "paying a living wage and not exploiting the poor".

Bishop Phillip said: "A relationship with God cannot be divorced from relationships with our neighbours, especially those in need."

During the Good Friday service, to be held at the city's International Convention Centre, the Rev Phillip Pottet, an expert on economic justice and poverty issues and the general secretary of the ? Council of Churches, will be guest speaker.

Organised by the Dio? Council of Churches, the e? described as the largest ? denominational gathering on ? ban's Easter calendar, will be ? at least 3 500 people.

It will be followed by the ? tional silent procession from ? ICC to the city hall.

Forgiveness and reconciliation

It was a very special situation to walk through the city centre in Durban on Good Friday and remember the crucifixion of Christ. My husband, Philip Potter, gave the message. I stood with him, a black man, who had to take a lot of blows for his courageous stands in the anti-racism struggle of the World Council of Churches.

Together we saw people queuing in this sunny morning for forgiveness and reconciliation. Who was I, a German person, to grant forgiveness to South Africans? I wondered what amount of violence and suffering was present in that moment. This silent hour made the act of penitence more meaningful than ever, indeed it rescued it for me from shallow practice.

For a moment I wished I could have stood on the other side, with the people seeking forgiveness. It made another person of me. The sacredness of suffering clearly spoke to me about the sacredness of life, when I looked at these women, men and children. Not often can one touch the depth of the act of penitence.

Years later, I participated in Germany in a situation where two lay people shared with me as clergy the act of penitence. Immediately I thought of Good Friday in Durban. Tears came to my eyes, remembering all the suffering of the South African people and my unwilling/willing participation in their oppression as German people during the apartheid times.

Good Friday in Durban brought back to me the message of self-giving, suffering and forgiveness. As many times before, it was in South Africa that I understood better what the gospel is about.

Bishop Bärbel Wartenberg-Potter
Lübeck, Germany

Commitment

The poor of our land cry:
"We are being crucified by poverty.
When we appeal to government and business, they say,
    wait, your economic slice will arrive soon.
How much longer are we expected to wait,
    before we can get a healthy slice of the economic pie.
How long must we wait for a better life?"

O God, hear the cries of our people, and help us to:
    transform unjust policies which contribute to the suffering
        of the poor;
    protect our people from global economic injustice;
    hasten the just distribution of resources;
    and improve the quality of life for all our people.

We commit ourselves to work with you
    to bring about a just economic system for all humanity.

END VIOLENCE AGA
Makuphele ukuhluku
kwabesifazane

INKON
Good

13 April

Kingsme
Old Fort

Diakonia
Diakonia Centre, 2
PO Box 61341, Bisl
Fax: (031) 305-248

INTER-PERSONAL VIOLENCE

Inter-personal violence was one of apartheid's most destructive legacies, and one of the most difficult to confront. South Africa remained one of the most violent countries in the world, with women and children paying the highest price. One woman was killed by her partner every six days. Child abuse had reached horrific proportions. The scourge of HIV/AIDS was both a contributing factor and the result of this violence. One in nine people in South Africa was living with HIV.

And so it seemed right to focus on the theme *'End Violence against Women'* at the Good Friday service held on 13 April, offering an opportunity to remember all those women who had been raped, killed or injured in domestic violence, and to pray that men would repent of violence against women.

END VIOLENCE AGAINST WOMEN

The service began at the Kingsmead Cricket Stadium. A group of twelve women carried sticks on their heads into the stadium, as a symbol of the burden of violence they bear. As stories were told showing some of the ways in which women are physically and psychologically abused, and how this is caused by the way our society is structured, women prostrated themselves in front of the horrors of rape, assault and structural violence perpetrated against women.

While Anglican Bishop Rubin Phillip read an adaptation of verses from the prophet Isaiah and a saxophone lament was played by Bernhard Kreft – a young German intern with Diakonia – women lashed the sticks together into a cross, as their sisters knelt in prayer. Bishop Purity Malinga of the Methodist Church preached a powerful and moving sermon.

As the rising sun streamed across the stadium, women carried the cross out into the streets of the city. Church leaders led a silent procession through the streets of Durban behind a banner with the message *'End Violence against Women'*. At the front of the City Hall the cross was raised up and a wreath was placed on it as a sign of mourning for all women who have suffered violence.

The congregation was invited to commit themselves to do whatever they could to bring to an end violence against women. As a sign of their commitment, people turned to their neighbour, placed the palms of their hands together with those of their neighbour, and said: *'We pledge to end violence against women.'* Each person attending the service received a prayer card with a list of organisations involved in assisting abused and violated women.

Call to worship

Come to the living God
    Come to stand alongside women who suffer
    Come to struggle with those who seek
        freedom
    Come to resist all that offends God's justice
Come to Jesus as he hangs on the cross
Come to the living, disturbing God

Stories spoken by women who have suffered violence

"I came out of the cottage to chop wood for the fire. As I walked to the pile of logs, this man jumped out of the shadows and dragged me into the house, threatening me with my axe. He pushed me into the bathroom, threw me on the floor and raped me. I was afraid he would kill me. But he left me lying there and ran away. I managed to free myself and tried to phone for help, but he had cut the wires. I walked to the nearest house down the road. They telephoned the police and my friends, who went searching for the man. They found him and arrested him. I had to go to court to say what happened. I found that very difficult. He's in prison now, but I still feel frightened. It's hard for me to trust anyone."

"Psychological abuse also leaves scars. I know, because I suffered mental abuse for 25 years. This kind of abuse is practised in several ways. One is to isolate you from your family, so that you become totally dependent on the abuser. I could probably count on one hand the number of times I visited, or was visited by, my family. I was told that if they ever appeared again, I would be assaulted. I asked my family to please leave me alone. Another practice is to belittle you to such an extent that you lose all confidence and self respect. I took it because I had become totally dependent. The terrible thing about mental abuse is that you gradually hand over the control of your life, your very self, to your partner."

"For 17 years of my married life, my husband has been assaulting me every weekend. Last year, one of my relatives told me about the court interdict. I went to court and applied for it. The messenger of the court served him with a summons at work. When he came back from work that day, he was drunk and started assaulting me until the next morning. For the whole week, I couldn't move or go out of the house, but when he came back from work, he would demand food. Because of the injuries I sustained that day, I can't hold heavy stuff and I can't do the washing for my family."

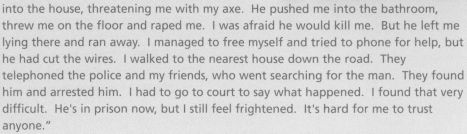

Creating artwork for Good Friday services

It was always special to be given the task of creating artwork for the Good Friday service. The themes were often quite challenging in terms of image-making but it always worked out well in the end!

Different service themes had different aspects for me. The 2001 theme *'End Violence against Women'* probably meant the most to me, spiritually. I think I had the greatest freedom with my artwork. And I was thrilled to be so much more involved in the actual service with the special ritual we devised.

From a creative aspect there were certain posters that worked out beautifully – thanks to Maria Criticos. It is always so good working with Maria because she can transform all my scribbles into a great composition! For example posters of 1993, 1994, 1996, 2003 and 2006 – and much earlier 1989.

I particularly enjoy story-telling, so the painted cross gave a marvellous opportunity for that. It was like extending the imagery of so many of the posters I made for Diakonia. I believe it made and still makes an impact because people can relate to the didactic aspect.

Over the years, there were two instances where I was disappointed that Diakonia didn't approve of my ideas.

Dina Cormick

YINHLABALUHIDE yabazalwane bamabandla ahlukene abelibhekise eCity Hall. KWESINCANE nguBishop Purity Malinga obethula intshumayelo yakhe enkonzweni yePhasika ebiseKingsmead. Isiqubulo sale nkonzo besithi: "Makuphele ukuhlukunyezwa kwabesifazane." Izithombe ngu-ABE PHUNGULA. Funda nasekhasini 7. ILANGA 16-18/04/2001

ACT AGAINST VIOLENCE AGAINST WOMEN

nisaa INSTITUTE FOR WOMEN'S DEVELOPMENT

Healing the Wounds of Society

Selapha ukulimala komphakathi

Preacher:
The Revd Hawu Mbatha

Inkonzo yePhasika · Good Friday Service
Durban Exhibition Centre
Friday 29 March 2002 · 6.15am

Diakonia Council of Churches · Diakonia Centre, 20 St. Andrews Street, Durban 4001 · PO Box 61341, Bishopsgate 4008
Phone: 031 310-3500 · Fax: 031 310-3502 · E-mail: diak@iafrica.com

CHRISTIANS UNITE AGAINST RACISM

The World Conference Against Racism (WCAR) took place in Durban from 31 August to 7 September 2001. Local and international churches played a significant role at the event. The conference was an opportunity to strengthen the relationship between the international ecumenical movement and South African churches.

As well as having delegates both to the non-governmental (NGO) Forum and the main conference, Diakonia assisted the WCC delegates in a number of ways. Diakonia, the WCC and the SACC hosted a special service at Methodist Central City Mission on 31 August. Anglican Bishop Rubin Phillip in his sermon said: *"Christians must acknowledge and confess that racism and intolerance still exist in the church."* The service was followed by a candlelight procession to the City Hall, where approximately 1 000 people committed themselves to work to end racism.

ANOTHER WORLD IS POSSIBLE

South Africa was by no means immune to these challenges. In April 1994 – the month of the first democratic elections – an international agreement had been signed in Marrakesh, Morocco, opening the way to the founding of the World Trade Organisation (WTO). As a founding WTO member, South Africa had to reduce the tariff barriers which had protected goods for so long, opening South Africa's manufacturing sector to international competition.

Two years later, the government had adopted the GEAR (Growth, Employment & Redistribution) macro-economic policy. While GEAR produced a turn-around in economic growth, this masked a deeper problem: jobless growth. Statistics South Africa reported that one million jobs were lost between February and September 2001 alone, pushing the expanded unemployment rate, including discouraged job seekers, up to 41.5%.

There had been significant achievements by government. But, feeding on poverty and the lack of a clear government strategy, the HIV/AIDS pandemic had exploded.

If another world was to be realised, South Africans from all walks of life needed to be active in bringing about change.

HEALING THE WOUNDS OF SOCIETY

The Good Friday service on 29 March focussed on the theme *'Healing the Wounds of Society.'*

In some ways, it was a follow-up to the WCAR held in Durban the previous August/September. That conference had highlighted the wounds caused by racism and other forms of discrimination, and showed that much healing was still needed. This reality had been accentuated by the events a few days later in New York and Washington and the resultant *'War on Terror'* started by the USA, which was to have such tragic and ongoing consequences.

More than 3 000 people attended the Good Friday service at the Durban Exhibition Centre. An inspiring sermon by the Revd Hawu Mbatha of the Uniting Reformed Church reflected on the wounds caused by racism, political and domestic violence and HIV/AIDS. He pinpointed the challenges these issues raise for Christians.

The cross used at the service and carried through the streets of Durban was the cross designed and painted by Dina Cormick to be used at an earlier Good Friday service in 1991, depicting scenes from the time when KwaZulu-Natal was torn apart by violence that killed at least ten thousand and made thousands more homeless.

A unique feature of the service was the invitation to those who had suffered trauma to come forward and receive a blessing from church leaders on the steps of the City Hall. Thereafter, they were given the opportunity to receive suggestions about where they could receive further counselling from English and isiZulu-speaking counsellors. An overwhelming number of people responded to this invitation. A list of *'Resources for healing'* was published in the service programme.

THE DAY THE WORLD CHANGED

The events which took place in New York, Washington and close to Pittsburgh in the United States of America (USA) on 11 September 2001 cast a shadow over the lives of people all over the world. By the end of 2001, the death toll of 'revenge' attacks in Afghanistan had already overtaken the number of people killed at the World Trade Centre in New York.

Civil war raged in several African countries and HIV/AIDS tightened its deadly grip on our continent. The Israeli-Palestinian conflict worsened. In city centres and rural villages, images of destruction and suffering flashed across television and computer screens, reinforcing our membership of the 'global village'.

It is important to consider how global economic inequalities provide the context in which violence and terror flourish. Globalisation in its current form had widened the gap between the haves and have-nots. Multinational companies and international financial institutions were sometimes more powerful than governments. New computer technology had enabled speculators to move almost unhindered across the globe in search of profit, ignoring the effects on people, economies and the environment.

Was it possible to link people and cultures in ways that were not destructive?

Blessing

We affirm that our nation needs
    healing and wholeness
        black and white
        women and men
        old and young
        parents and children
        rich and poor
        refugee and citizen.

    God bless Africa,
    guard her people
    guide her leaders
    and grant her peace

Now God's home is with all people!
God shall live with them and they
    will be God's people.
God will be their God and will
    wipe away all tears from
    their eyes.
There will be no more death, no
    more grief or crying or pain.
The old has gone and the new
    has come.

In silence lies unity

The first Good Friday service of Diakonia that I attended was in 2002. The theme that year was *'Healing the Wounds of Society.'* The impressions I have from that early morning service were more or less the same as those that I experienced in services the following years.

The first experience I had was the greatness of being part of God's church – to be part of this ecumenical gathering that is so much bigger and so much more representative than just the white NG Kerk (Dutch Reformed Church) I was used to. Suddenly I was part of thousands of other Christians, from different churches, different backgrounds, different races, cultures and languages. It was wonderful to be absorbed by this group – to sing together, to pray together, and to listen to God's word together.

The second experience had to do with the richness of the liturgy and the theme(s). The liturgy helped to lead the whole group in focussing on God, and the themes that were presented by the speakers year by year were always very practical and challenging.

The most significant experience for me was, however, the march to the City Hall. To march in silence through this city that is normally so busy and so noisy, made it look completely different. It looked peaceful, quiet and full of expectation. Walking with all those Christians through the streets helped me to realise that we as Christians can make a difference. It helped me to find hope – hope for a city and people with wounds, with women and children that are abused, with so much poverty.

To walk in silence like that created a tremendous feeling of unity between us – no words were necessary to explain our combined prayer and hope and love for all of God's people.

Revd Dr Anné Verhoef

Children on the Cross
Izingane Esiphambanweni

Inkonzo yePhasika · Good Friday Service
Durban Exhibition Centre
Friday · 18 April 2003 · 6.15am

Diakonia Council of Churches · Diakonia Centre, 20 St. Andrew's Street, Durban 4001
PO Box 61341, Bishopsgate 4008 · Phone: 031 310-3500 · Fax: 031 310-3502 · E-mail: the.director@diakonia.org.za

SIGNS OF HOPE AS POVERTY DEEPENS

At the beginning of February 2003, thousands of delegates from around the world had gathered at the second World Social Forum in Porto Alegre, Brazil, to discuss *'Global Justice and Life after Capitalism.'*

As the USA and the United Kingdom (UK) prepared to invade Iraq that February, millions of people across the globe – from Chicago to Durban, Mexico City to Manila and London – gathered to protest. Governments, including that of South Africa, also stood firm against the invasion.

The extent of the protests took the USA and the UK by surprise. And the correctness of the protestors' position was upheld when the war began. The horrific carnage of innocent civilians shook even the most stern-hearted. No weapons of mass destruction – the ostensible justification for war – were found.

International peace protests against the invasion of Iraq were not isolated events. Rather, they were part of a sustained social movement that had been gathering momentum in the previous few years. In South Africa, peace protestors included the landless, unemployed and AIDS activists.

Unemployment and poverty had been rising. Slow economic growth and low investment had led to job losses and a decline in the quality of jobs. Poor South Africans had been hit with the highest rise in living costs in thirty years. Spiralling food prices made a large contribution to this increase. The majority of South Africans simply could not cope with any price increases.

IT DOESN'T HAVE TO BE *LIKE THIS*!

The participation of so many South Africans, including many church people, in the World Summit on Sustainable Development held in Johannesburg in September 2002 was part of the action to bring about the change needed. For many, it was the first time that issues around ecology, the degradation of the environment, alternative energy sources and the threats to food security had been raised in the context of the unjust economic system of the world. It was also an opportunity to hear the world debates about the very term *'sustainable development'* and what it really meant.

At a Diakonia seminar on 13 March 2003, clergy and lay people were challenged to consider how the economy could be restrucured so that it catered for the poor and the marginalised. The seminar was based on the recently-published book, *'It doesn't have to be LIKE THIS'* by economist Margaret Legum, who spoke about her theories and practices of alternative approaches. Margaret headed up the South African New Economics (SANE) network and offered clear alternatives to the current way of operating the national economy.

CHILDREN ON THE CROSS

Children had borne the brunt of rising poverty. Research revealed that a quarter of South Africa's children were stunted due to malnutrition. Seventy percent lived in poverty. As HIV/AIDS took its toll, more and more child-headed households eked out a miserable existence in isolation from their communities.

It was in this context that Diakonia decided on the theme *'Children on the Cross'* for the Good Friday service on 18 April 2003.

A particular feature of the service was the presence, among the more than 3 000 worshippers, of members of the ecumenical Christian community of the City of Bremen, Germany, who were in Durban during April to strengthen their ties with the Diakonia Council of Churches.

The City of Durban is a sister City of Bremen. Different sectors – including business, artists and sportspeople – have exchanged visits to strengthen this city partnership.

The German religious leaders took an active part in the Good Friday service, which they found particularly memorable. Diakonia is glad to share their story, and affirms this ecumenical partnership with the churches in Bremen.

Prayer

O Christ
you go hungry and homeless
as the children of the world are denied food

O Christ
you suffer the injustice of beatings and abuse
in you the children of the world cringe away
   terrified

O Christ
you hold your arms wide on the cross
and the children of the world bear the pain
   and scream

O Christ
you hear their tears, you share their tears
for you weep all the tears of the world

O Christ
by your suffering awaken us to the suffering of
   children
by your pain challenge us to transform society
by your resurrection help us to work for a world
      where despair will be changed to hope
      where pain will be changed to joy
      where tears will be changed to laughter.

Taking God's message out to the world

Very early in the morning, our delegation gets up and prepares to take part in the Good Friday service and procession organised every year by the Diakonia Council of Churches. An experience awaits us which will be etched deeply into us, and which will be one of the highlights of our partnership journey. Here are some impressions which live in me even after more than five years.

The cross of Good Friday, the cross of Jesus Christ, is carried outdoors, into the public spaces of the great city. No longer is it enshrined in church buildings. Two services take place this morning, in the Exhibition Centre and in front of the City Hall. From the one place to the other an impressive procession moves with the cross. The message of the church has political consequences for the city, for the world. That cannot be ignored.

Children are intimately involved during the whole event. It is *their* service. Some of them (pupils of St Francis College, Mariannhill) have painted the big mural on the wall behind the lectern. In bright colours and significant symbols their risks, their hopes, their life beneath the cross is expressed. This makes a very strong impression. Children and young people sing in wonderful choirs.

Children talk about their experiences, characterised by poverty, threats, violence and rape. Children carry the cross, which they themselves have made, into the service. Children read the United Nations' Children's Manifesto. The service doesn't just talk *about* children, but *with* them; and children themselves say what is important to them and what is a burden to them. In this way the whole service is an excellent demonstration of what is written on the huge banner: '*Put Children First.*'

The ecumenical community of the churches in Durban takes visible form with the participation of many congregations in this service. The bright colours of the different robes proclaim that praise of the Lord and service within society must be done together. The bible passages are read in English, isiZulu and Afrikaans. The Director of the Diakonia Council of Churches, Paddy Kearney, leads the service in a calm way that unites the different denominations.

Priscilla McKay, Director of Child and Family Welfare, gives an excellent sermon in which she names the problems of children in our society as clearly as needs saying, and in which she points directly to the tasks of church and society if the slogan '*Put Children First*' is to be made a reality. We would like to hear such clear words more often from our churches in Germany. Moving prayers are offered by Bishop Rubin Phillip, Noreen Ramsden, Cardinal Wilfrid Napier and the Revd Hawu Mbatha, highlighting the sermon. Not only the children in South Africa are included in the prayers, but also the children in Iraq, where war had just broken out.

The procession with the cross through the streets of Durban makes the decisive Christian message clear. The cross belongs in the heart of the city; everyone stands beneath the cross; everyone carries the burden of the cross; nobody belongs at the top or at the bottom. Both children and Mayor Obed Mlaba put the cross on their backs. This conveys a strong symbolic meaning.

We, the guests from Bremen, are included in a very friendly manner. We are welcomed during the service. We carry the banner:'*Put Children First.*' We take part by offering a prayer in front of the City Hall. We join in the singing. We feel completely part of the whole service.

Finally, Church Leaders distribute the Children's Manifesto and flowers to the children, and then among all who take part in the service – a beautiful gesture which helps us all to leave with courage in our hearts.

All in all, the whole service convincingly and impressively conveys the mission statement of the work of the Diakonia Council of Churches:

> '*Our core purpose is to participate with our member churches and organisations in God's work of transforming society and its environment so that the fullness of life promised by Christ may become a reality for all.*'

Precisely this is our experience with the Good Friday service, containing within itself the promise and wonder of Easter.

Revd Martin Hausmann, Bremen
Member of delegation present in Durban in 2003
from Diakonia's partners in Bremen, Germany
Oekumenische Initiative Bremen

Life through the Cross
Siyophila ngeSiphambano

Inkonzo yePhasika · Good Friday Service
Friday · 9 April 2004 · 6.15am

Durban Exhibition Centre

Sculpture by Zamu Guineda, 2003

Diakonia Council of Churches · Diakonia Centre, 20 St. Andrew's Street, Durban 4001
PO Box 61341, Bishopsgate 4008 · Phone: 031 310-3500 · Fax: 031 310-3502 · E-mail: the.director@diakonia.org.za

CHALLENGES OF THE FUTURE

South Africa in 2004 was a very different place from the South Africa which tentatively reached out to freedom in 1994.

Ten years earlier, massacres, assassinations, solitary confinement and torture were the order of the day. Politically motivated violence tore communities apart.

No-one expected this violence to end so suddenly and so completely. Yet what was experienced in 2004, and for most of the previous ten years, was peace. It was not perfect. South Africa still suffered from terrifying amounts of criminal and domestic violence, but the politically motivated violence of the past was over.

There was of course much more to be done. South Africa still suffered from high levels of economic inequalities. Chronic poverty had its roots in unemployment. Women and African people suffered the highest rates of unemployment. The quality of the services provided and communities' ability to sustain access to them remained an area for concern.

But there could be no doubt that the foundations had been laid. South Africa had a strong economy. Wealth was being created. The challenge was to find a way of distributing it more fairly and justly.

A SIGNIFICANT YEAR

The year since the previous Good Friday service was in many ways a significant one in the history of Diakonia.

The Economic Justice Programme moved ahead with energy and purpose, as the organisation's first priority, with its comprehensive programme of education, reflection and action on economic justice.

For the first time in its history, Diakonia mounted a major programme on environmental issues, with the Social Justice Season in August on the theme *'God's Gift: The Earth, our Home'* offering bible studies and awareness-raising exposure visits, as well as practical ways in which church people could take action.

From now on, environmental and economic justice would be seen as two faces of the same major problem facing not only South Africa, but the world.

PADDY KEARNEY ANNOUNCES HIS RETIREMENT

2003 marked the end of an era for Diakonia. In August, pioneer director Paddy Kearney went on a long-overdue sabbatical leave of six months. During this period he decided that the time was right for him to retire from the organisation, after 28 years of service. He had set up and directed Diakonia, oversaw the transformation to the Diakonia Council of Churches and directed the 'new' agency for nine years.

In his message for the year's Annual Report published mid-2004, Bishop Rubin Phillip, then Chairperson of the organisation, wrote:

> *"I would like to give thanks for the outstanding and dedicated ministry of our founder director, Paddy Kearney. We give thanks for this outstanding servant of God whose contributions to Diakonia and the struggle for peace, justice and transformation in South Africa will long be remembered.*

> *"The appointment of Nomabelu Mvambo-Dandala as the new director from 1 July 2004 is to be welcomed. Having served in Diakonia for many years, including as deputy director, and given her leadership gifts, she is well positioned to lead Diakonia into the future."*

The year under review ended with the sudden and peaceful death of Archbishop-Emeritus Denis Hurley OMI – the great visionary whose inspiration was behind the founding of Diakonia in 1976. It was, then, perhaps particularly fitting that the 2003 Good Friday service should have as its theme *'Life through the Cross'*.

LIFE THROUGH THE CROSS

In April 2004, people all over the country were celebrating South Africa's first ten years of freedom and democracy.

The Good Friday service on 9 April was also celebratory, with solemn procession, music and dance, flowers and candles. Thanks were given for blessings already received through sufferings endured. Hopes and prayers were expressed for the future, with strength to face life's challenges.

Moving stories were told by people who had discovered new life through experiences offered by Diakonia's programmes. The congregation joined with them in affirming that God does indeed bring *'life through the cross'* of poverty and unemployment, HIV/AIDS, intolerance, violence and powerlessness. Through a message from Cardinal Wilfrid Napier, through readings, prayers and songs, through a small wooden cross handed to each person present, the spirit of life in all its fullness was proclaimed.

As people streamed out of the Exhibition Centre, the cross was carried through the city centre streets by groups representing the work of Diakonia and its member churches in overcoming the challenges of the day and bringing hope to so many.

At the City Hall steps, the cross was covered in flowers by members of the congregation in the ancient Christian ceremony, reminding believers of the life that comes through the cross of pain and suffering. As it was lifted for all to see, a commitment was made to continue to work for a more just society of peace and equality, healing and light.

This was the 19th Good Friday service, and the last to be led by retiring director Paddy Kearney, who had initiated the tradition in 1985 when a group of men and one woman, Albertina Sisulu, was held in Durban Central Prison while being tried on charges of treason.

Prayer

God of power,
God of people,
You are the life of all that lives,
 energy that fills the earth,
 vitality that brings to birth,
 the impetus toward making whole
  whatever is bruised or broken.
In You we grow to know the truth
 that sets all creation free.
You are the song the whole earth sings,
 the promise liberation brings.
Fill us with your life, your energy, your vitality,
 that we may work with You
  to make all people whole.
Free us to live your truth,
 to sing your song,
 to bring your liberation,
  now and forever.

2004

Icons of reconciliation

Leading Diakonia's Good Friday street procession for several years has been a special privilege for me. Accompanying me was the Revd Lawrence Mthethwa. As a white ordained woman and a black ordained man, we cut iconic figures of reconciliation across the gender, race and denominational divide. In that sense we embodied the values of the Diakonia Council of Churches.

To walk before the people of God was always a humbling experience. It was also an awkward experience: I often wanted to grab someone else from the side of the road and say *"you carry the cross"*. Actually we did not carry it. Each year different groups of people were chosen to carry the cross, reflecting Diakonia's commitment to ecumenism.

The annual procession was divided into "Stages of the Cross" and each small community would carry the cross for a portion of the journey. Behind Lawrence and I there was always a deep and solemn sense of awe emanating from the group.

A major event in the KwaZulu-Natal churches' calendar, the services extend into the public space the vision and witness of the church. For individual people participating, it is a heartening experience to be part of this.

Revd Bernice Stott

GOOD NEWS FOR THE POOR

IZINDABA EZINHLE KWABAMPOFU

Photograph by Paul Weinberg ©

Good Friday Service * Inkonzo yePhasika
Durban City Hall
Friday 25 March 2005 * 6.15 am

Diakonia Council of Churches, 20 St Andrew's Street, Durban. P.O. Box 61341, Bishopsgate, 4008
Phone: 031-310 3500, Fax: 031-310 3502, Email: the.director@diakonia.org.za

POVERTY DEEPENS

The textile and clothing sectors used to be the largest employers in KwaZulu-Natal. They provided 24 000 jobs in more than 500 firms and contributed R4 billion to the province's gross domestic product. But 8 600 of these jobs were lost between 2003 and the beginning of 2005.

In 2004, South Africa recorded its highest economic growth since 1996. Yet jobs continued to be shed at an alarming rate. As unemployment bit deeper, more people looked to social grants in order to survive. While the government claimed a high rate of delivery, bureaucratic red tape delayed or denied access to many.

Unemployment and poverty both contribute to ill-health, and made private health care unaffordable for the majority of South Africans. Despite continued pressure from civil society organisations, the rollout of anti-retroviral treatment for people living with AIDS remained very slow.

The struggle against apartheid succeeded because ordinary citizens asserted their rights. The problems of unemployment, poverty and disease in South Africa would not be solved by government proclamation. They would be resolved through all sectors of society working together, particularly at local level.

TRANSFORMATION

Transformation was in the air in 2004/5. All around were change and new beginnings.

Everyone in South Africa, it seemed, was assessing progress made in the first ten years of democracy: evaluation was also in the air. But an organisational evaluation carried out at this time was about more than that. It was an attempt to reorientate the organisation to the new realities of life in South Africa, more particularly in the eThekwini Municipality where Diakonia works.

Diakonia's Council accepted the findings of the evaluation at the beginning of June 2004 and a process was initiated to put the findings into effect. With a new vision and mission statement, the organisation had started on a new road, with a renewed sense of purpose.

VISION
A transformed society actively working for social justice.

MISSION STATEMENT
In partnership with our member churches and organisations we are inspired by our Christian faith to play a transformative role enabling people to take responsibility for their lives and to promote prophetic action on social justice issues.

GOOD NEWS FOR THE POOR

The slogan *'Good News for the Poor'* was chosen as a theme for 2005 against the backdrop of continuing poverty. The Good Friday service on 25 March was the first major occasion in a year of relating to various aspects of the struggle to *'Make Poverty History'*. It was decided to use the same theme for the Social Justice Season in August.

Bishop Purity Malinga's strong words at the Good Friday service set the tone for the organisation's focus on poverty. In her challenging address she reminded the large gathering filling the City Hall that Christians represent Christ in the world and Christ continues his mission through us.

The colourful procession carried the cross around the outside of the building to the steps at the front, where the ancient ceremony of flowering the cross inspired the congregation anew with hope and faith.

GOOD NEWS FOR THE POOR

IZINDABA EZINHLE KWABAMPOFU

Good Friday Service - Inkonzo yePhasika
Durban City Hall
Friday 25 March 2005 - 6.15am

Responsive Prayer

Loving God, we believe you are the God of the poor and that poverty includes being hungry, unemployed and orphaned, living on a pension or grant, meagre earnings for arduous and hazardous work, ill health, anxiety and stress, and the absence of power, worsened for women by unequal gender relations.
      Loving God, we hold up to you all those living in poverty.

We believe that God wants all people to live a dignified life and engage in meaningful work, that workers should receive fair wages, and that those who possess more resources and skills must share them in neighbourly love with those who have less.
      Loving God, open our eyes to the deep needs of those who are poor.

We believe that the challenge of fighting poverty does not lie solely with governments, but that faith-based organisations are ideally positioned to address it, with their human and financial resources.
      Loving God, challenge us to see ways in which we can work against poverty.

We renew our commitment to be in solidarity with the poor and to work against any form of injustice. We commit ourselves to put our faith into action and to demonstrate our faith in practical ways, so that together we can overcome the scourge of poverty.
      Loving God, in your mercy hear our prayer and strengthen us in our commitment.

Based on extracts from statements on poverty by Diakonia's member churches

Good News for the Poor
Extract of sermon by Bishop Purity Malinga, Methodist Church

2005

We all have images of poor people in this country and this city. Not only that, but some of us are the poor. While the poor come from all backgrounds, it is a fact that the poor in our country are mostly black, living in rural areas or inner cities, mostly women and children. They are the unemployed, the homeless, the landless and refugees. There are poor people who, while they work hard, earn very little, such as farm workers, domestic workers, etc. One can go on. Whoever they are, the poor are amongst us and cannot be wished away or ignored.

BISHOP Zeblon Nqcamu of the United Apostolic Church and Bishop Purity Malinga of the Methodist Church are two of the religious leaders who will lead the 20th Annual Diakonia Council of Churches' Good Friday Service tomorrow, beginning at the Durban City Hall at 6:15am. The service will be followed by a procession through the streets of Durban
PICTURE: STRU MFEKA

Day in and day out the poor men, women and children of our nation hope for the good news, as they go up and down begging, searching for job opportunities, selling this and that, trying to make ends meet. The news they get every day is *"no jobs, you are not good enough, go away – sorry we can't help you."* They suffer ridicule and rejection from all angles. As this happens their self-esteem and human dignity get eroded. Some feel humiliated and, in turn, humiliate those at their disposal. Others give up on life and destroy themselves with drugs and alcohol.

Our gathering under the cross this morning is to declare that there is good news for the poor in Jesus Christ. In his birth, life and ministry, Jesus revealed to us the God who cares and takes sides with the poor and oppressed.

The message of good news to and for the poor did not end on the cross, because Jesus did not end on the cross. On the third day he rose, and lives forever. The message of good news for the poor is to be heard wherever there are Christian people, because that is what Christ calls us to proclaim. We represent him in the world, and he continues his mission through us.

Christians, individually and collectively, cannot afford to be indifferent about what poverty is doing to our nation. As the rich keep getting richer, the poor are literally dying of starvation and HIV/AIDS. The situation in our communities has reached crisis level.

With this service, we as member churches of Diakonia are declaring solidarity with the poor, and our commitment to fighting poverty. The churches' preferential option for the poor is practical, and some churches are already doing practical things to change the lives of the poor.

As individual Christians let us be moved to make a difference. Then collectively we will make a big diference. The love of Christ who died for us must propel us to live for him and to proclaim good news to and for the poor in our words and deeds.

Unity in faith and action

The suffering of Jesus on the cross remains abstract and meaningless for those who are unaware of sin and its effects. The genius of the Diakonia Good Friday services is using various themes to point out and conscientise us to the effects of our individual and collective sin. Our attention has been drawn over the years to poverty, women and child abuse, discrimination and prejudice, etc. We have been reminded of the great love of God who chose to suffer on the cross to bring full life to all created order.

I have left each of these services with a strong resolve, as a follower of Jesus Christ, to work hard towards ending the suffering of God's people. I have been challenged to speak out and act against the injustices of our time.

To me personally, the experience of carrying the heavy cross through the city has given me a glimpse of what Jesus experienced. That and much, much more suffering for my salvation! The service always leaves me amazed at the love of God.

It is at this service that our unity in faith and action as Christians is expressed. The message of the cross brings us together and challenges us all to stand for what our Lord stood for. I trust that Diakonia will continue to lift up the cross and its meaning through these services.

Bishop Purity Malinga
Methodist Church
Natal Coastal District

Crucified by Poverty

Preacher: Presiding Bishop Ivan Abrahams

Ubethelelwe Ngobumpofu

Inkonzo yePhasika · Good Friday Service
Friday · 14 April 2006 · 6.15am

Sahara Kingsmead Cricket Stadium — cnr Old Fort and NMR Ave

Diakonia Council of Churches · Diakonia Centre, 20 Diakonia Avenue, Durban 4001
PO Box 61341, Bishopsgate 4008 · Phone: 031 310-3500 · Fax: 031 310-3502 · E-mail: the.director@diakonia.org.za · Website: www.diakonia.org.za

DIAKONIA — THIRTY YEARS OF SERVICE AND ACTION FOR JUSTICE — 1976–2006

In 2006 Diakonia celebrated thirty years of service and action for justice, with the theme *"Never again will human rights be forgotten."*

A week of celebration culminated in a gala dinner on the anniversary of 25 March 1976, the day on which the churches in Durban came together at a time of great injustice and repression to form an ecumenical agency that would help Christians – and all those of good will – to speak out and to act prophetically as the evil of apartheid strengthened its grip.

It was a time to go down memory lane. Many who took part in the wide variety of events had been faithful participants in the annual Good Friday services since 1985.

Diakonia's work has always been set in the context of its time. By 2006 it was no longer institutionalised apartheid as the backdrop and focus, but poverty.

A key event of the week in March was the launch of Diakonia's publication *'The Oikos Journey',* which helped churches to grapple with the fact that the economy was also in the hands of institutions and people driven by self-interest and greed. Poverty is not an accident, nor is unemployment. And as it deepens, so does the destruction of the environment, of God's world, our only home. The work of both economic and environmental justice is crucial for those who worship a God who loves and cares for the world and all its people.

And so the Good Friday service three weeks later on 14 April had as its theme: *"Crucified by Poverty".*

The voices of the poor themselves were heard. The preacher at the Sahara Kingsmead Cricket Stadium, was Methodist Presiding Bishop Ivan Abrahams, who had attended the World Social Forum in Nairobi.

After the procession through the streets of Durban to the steps of the City Hall – to the solemn tolling of the bell of St Paul's Anglican Church – the flowering of the cross ceremony once again gave people an opportunity to place a flower onto the cross before it was lifted up for all to see – a reminder that Christ overcame the cross, as we will make poverty history. People joined in a commitment to hearing the cries of the poor and sharing resources, so that all may have life in all its fullness.

THE OIKOS JOURNEY

From 1994 a democratic government was in place in South Africa, which brought with it expectations of a better life. The establishment of a constitutional democracy was celebrated, with its stress on freedom from injustice, more equal opportunities and a better quality of life for all. However, the majority of people continued to live in poverty.

A Diakonia study group met for over a year to reflect on how the churches needed to respond. Inspired by the *'Kairos Document'* published in 1985 at the height of apartheid repression, which challenged the churches to get involved in God's call for a more just society, the study group prepared and Diakonia published *'The Oikos Journey.'*

'The Oikos Journey' starts with an introduction explaining why such a document was crucial at this point in South Africa's history. It then shares the voices of the poor as they tell their stories, and analyses the world economy and the South African economy in the light of globalisation and its destruction of the environment, before sharing thoughts on what economics does to people.

The document includes seven biblical principles about God's economy, which are presented simply and clearly, leading to four learnings about economics and ecology from *oikos.*

Finally, the challenge of the *oikos* journey is presented. Three levels of response are outlined: the welfare response of trying to meet people's immediate needs; the developmental response of helping people to empower themselves; and the prophetic response of challenging structures that entrench injustice and poverty. The document is a reminder of the values of the *oikos* community: hope, compassion, sharing, mutual support, equity and justice.

If we take *'The Oikos Journey'* seriously, God could indeed use us to change the lives of those living in poverty in South Africa.

Sermon Extract 'Crucified by Poverty'

by Presiding Bishop Ivan Abrahams, Methodist Church

This, like any other age, is an age of pilgrimage. God is forever inviting the church to join him as co-partners in mission on a journey of faith and hope. God calls us to go beyond 'what is' to 'what can be' – a vision of a *'new heaven and a new earth.'*

Many of the informal housing settlements of eThekwini are *'outside the city gates.'* These are the places where the poor live who don't experience the benefits of globalisation, privatisation and the market economy. It was outside the city gates that Jesus lived and died with the poor. If we want to meet Jesus today it has to be in ministry alongside those that society sacrifices on the altar of materialism and crucify by poverty.

Those 'outside the gates' have endless ways of speaking to us. They speak through their eloquent silence, their wounds and despair, but today they speak to us through Jesus in his spiritual agony, hunger and pain. Our theme *'Crucified by Poverty'* affirms Jesus' solidarity with the poor and God's struggle against poverty. Jesus, naked and thirsty on the cross, is the embodiment of all who are denied their basic human rights and dignity.

Poverty in a world of plenty is a scandal and an affront to God who is the Creator and Sustainer and Redeemer of the world. Poverty is in direct conflict with God's will for humanity. I am convinced that poverty anywhere is the enemy of prosperity every-where. It is not a mind full of theories but an empty, rumbling belly that is the recipe for a revolution. We need to go beyond resolutions and strategies to address hunger, because the poor cannot eat resolutions or strategies. We need partnership, collaboration and ministry that enters the world of those crucified by poverty.

We have celebrated the miracle of political emancipation. But we still have a long way to go to experience economic justice and a *'better life for all.'* Our struggle is not over until all have food security.

We are the people of the resurrection, we are prisoners of hope. We are a people who know that we cannot have Easter without Good Friday. We cannot have Christ without the cross. The cross is the symbol of God – a compassionate, loving God who identifies with human suffering. It is also God's instrument of salvation. No other faith speaks about a suffering God who opposes injustice and oppression. I want to challenge all of us this morning to become agents of transformation. A different world is possible and you and I are called to work towards that vision.

Walking the way of the Cross

To all followers of Christ, Good Friday is the highest point of our Lord's suffering followed by our highest point of joy and celebration, His resurrection.

As in any sphere of life, once one is chosen to lead there is always a question: *"Why me, Lord?"* This question always comes to me, each time Diakonia asks me to lead the Good Friday procession.

When I was in Jerusalem in 2005, our group of pilgrims requested me to lead the procession on the Via Dolorosa, the journey on which our Lord walked. I could feel tears rolling down my cheeks.

So all Good Fridays are very special to me. They bring back and refresh my memory of the day I knelt while touching the rock our Lord leaned on praying at Gethsemane. I followed the whole way of the cross to Calvary up to His tomb.

When Diakonia organises the Good Friday service in Durban and I walk in front leading the procession of the followers of Christ, the whole passion of Christ plays back in my mind like a film on the screen. I feel the heaviness of the cross Christ carried on his bruised shoulders. Each time I take a step forward in the proces-sion, I affirm *"I will go (do it, Lord), send me,"* (Isaiah 6:8) *"I will follow you."*

The scripture readings, the homily, the life experiences shared at the Good Friday service are enough to make one feel Christ's presence. *"Where two or three are gathered in My name, there I am in their midst."*

The silent procession accompanied by the tolling of St Paul's Church bell is always the last straw that breaks the camel's back: one cannot avoid dissolving into tears.

That is our Good Friday in Durban.

Revd Lawrence Mthethwa

A prayer to make poverty history

Christ our Lord,
your light shines into the shadows
and shows us where the obstacles
to change lie.

We know that often they are in our
own hearts,
in the way we live,
and in our daily choices
and actions.

Be with us, Lord Jesus Christ,
as we face your challenge
and learn how to live our lives
in love.

Heal, Reconcile and Build 1991

Never again will human rights be forgotten

Diakonia

Celebrating 30 years
of services to
Church & Community

1976 - 2006

Diakonia
Thirty Years of Service and Action for Justice
1976–2006
Never again will human rights be forgotten

Diakonia News

Diakonia

Celebrating
30 years
of service
to Church
& Community

1976
–
2006

YOUR VOTE IS
SECRET

YOUR VOTE IS
IMPORTANT
use it

Diakonia
working with the
church
in the struggle
for a just
and
democratic
South Africa

Christians Unite Against Racism
Amakresta Abambisene Ekuchitheni
Ukucwasana

SUSTAINABLE DEVELOPMENT
IS POSSIBLE!

WE OVERCOME THROUGH THE CROSS
Siyanqoba Ngesiphambano

Preacher: Bishop Rubin Phillip

Inkonzo yePhasika · Good Friday Service
Friday · 6 April 2007 · 6.15am
International Convention Centre (ICC)

TRANSFORMATION IN CHURCH AND SOCIETY

If Diakonia, in partnership with its member churches and organisations, is to carry out its mission of playing a transformative role, enabling people to take responsibility for their lives and to promote prophetic action on social justice issues, the organisation needs to keep reminding itself that Diakonia operates in a society that is constantly changing. And the church is also constantly changing.

But this is sometimes more difficult to see, and harder to accept. There is a sense in which much of the influence of the church is based on the notion that, in fact, it does not change: that it remains a beacon of unchanging, dependable stability in a world changing for the worse.

But, through its work with member churches since 1976, Diakonia knows that this is not so. Quiet revolutions have been seen in many member churches related to the society around them, as well as to their internal workings.

Diakonia believes that, thanks to the God in whose name the work is done, it has contributed much over the years to these changes, and remains committed to continuing the efforts for transformation.

To do this, it is necesssary to accurately understand what is happening in society in the context of the work, as well as in the church. Critical analysis and sound theology need to underpin everything. Diakonia works to put faith into action.

WE OVERCOME THROUGH THE CROSS

I n 2007 the backdrop of poverty, unemployment, crime, violence, HIV/AIDS, power struggles, corruption and environmental threats was still the context in which Diakonia and its member churches worked. But increasingly the churches were analysing the underlying causes of this suffering with tools such as *'The Oikos Journey'*.

The focus of the 2007 Good Friday service was on positive ways forward out of the suffering.

As nearly four thousand people from all walks of life sat in the darkened hall, a lone drum beat out a rhythm. From the darkness emerged the figure of the Christ, crowned with thorns, slowly and painfully carrying the cross towards Calvary. So began the 22nd ecumenical Good Friday service on 6 April, in the recently renamed Inkosi Albert Luthuli International Convention Centre.

In an atmosphere charged with the drama and tragedy of the occasion, dancers of the Flatfoot Dance Company accompanied the Christ-figure in dance and mime through the hall and up the steps, to the plaintive solo singing of the old spiritual *'Were you there when they crucified my Lord?'* As the cross was planted on the stage, the hall was plunged into darkness once more, signifying the death of Christ. The drum began its beat again and the lights slowly came up. Suddenly the scene was transformed. Dancers erupted across the stage in joyful movement, leaping and dancing their triumph at the empty cross, symbol that the crucified Christ had risen again.

We overcome through the cross, indeed. The clear message set the tone for the rest of a moving Good Friday service. Through prayer and song, through personal testimony from a self-help group member, and through the wise words of Bishop Rubin Phillip's sermon, the eventual victory of the cross was proclaimed – even over the terrible suffering of so many through poverty, unemployment, violence and HIV/AIDS.

Church leaders and others carried the cross through Durban's streets to the front of the City Hall, where the flowering of the cross was carried out, symbolically demonstrating faith in the resurrection of Christ and the overcoming of all suffering, pain and despair.

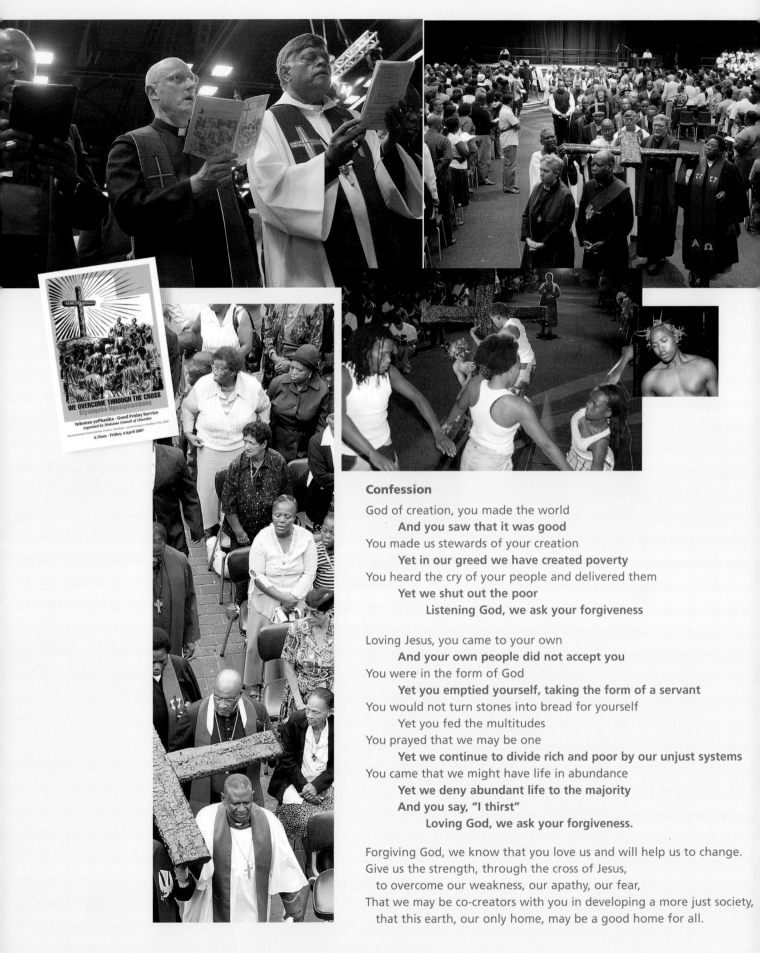

Confession

God of creation, you made the world
>   **And you saw that it was good**
You made us stewards of your creation
>   **Yet in our greed we have created poverty**
You heard the cry of your people and delivered them
>   **Yet we shut out the poor**
>>   **Listening God, we ask your forgiveness**

Loving Jesus, you came to your own
>   **And your own people did not accept you**
You were in the form of God
>   **Yet you emptied yourself, taking the form of a servant**
You would not turn stones into bread for yourself
>   **Yet you fed the multitudes**
You prayed that we may be one
>   **Yet we continue to divide rich and poor by our unjust systems**
You came that we might have life in abundance
>   **Yet we deny abundant life to the majority**
>   **And you say, "I thirst"**
>>   **Loving God, we ask your forgiveness.**

Forgiving God, we know that you love us and will help us to change.
Give us the strength, through the cross of Jesus,
   to overcome our weakness, our apathy, our fear,
That we may be co-creators with you in developing a more just society,
   that this earth, our only home, may be a good home for all.

2007

'Crucified by Poverty' march to mark Good Friday

The Diakonia Council of Churches held its Good Friday service at the ICC yesterday, followed by a march through the city streets to the Durban City Hall, during its 22nd annual celebration of Good Friday. The celebration focused on the theme 'Crucified by Poverty'. A year ago Diakonia published *The Oikos Journey*, a theological reflection on poverty and td the injustices in society, and focusing on the church's response to poverty and unemployment issues. eThekwini Mayor Obed MiMlaba (second from left) marched with the clerics. Photo: RAJESH JANTILAL

God – source of all creativity

The annual Good Friday service has become important in the ecumenical life of the church, as well as being a significant event in the city of Durban. It has been well supported since its inception. Demographically, ecumenically and socially, there is always a healthy representation.

Over the past few years, I have been privileged to take an active part in the service, which has become a highlight. Some aspects of the service are quite intriguing and, as such, have become meaningful to me.

The Good Friday service, whilst primarily a solemn commemoration of the death of Jesus, also affords a unique opportunity to reflect where we are as a community, a society and ultimately as a nation. In order to contextualise this, themes are carefully chosen to enable us to focus on the realities of our times.

At the heart of Jesus' ministry was the need for transformation. People are sometimes unaware of the magnitude of social ills. The Good Friday service provides a means of education. In order for the process of transformation to begin, the first step is for people to stay abreast of current issues. Christians need to move out of their comfort zones to a position where they are prepared to make sacrifices. This aspect is highlighted in the carefully prepared liturgies, where people are urged to make a commitment to becoming involved.

I am always heartened by the presentation of these services. Apart from having times of meditation, reflection, introspection and dedication, effective use is made of the arts. Music is, and will always be, an integral part of worship. However, dance, drama and poetry have also been used effectively to communicate messages of faith, hope and love. In doing this, Diakonia has engaged the services of professional arts practitioners as well as ordinary community-based people, who often share their stories in powerful ways.

The services are presented creatively, which in itself serves as a model. I have always felt that we need to explore creative ways of worshipping God as well as presenting the gospel. Watching a gripping dramatic piece or listening to an enchanting musical work moves people, sometimes much more than words uttered during a sermon. The memories of these moments also tend to linger much longer and can trigger a quicker response from people, which may ultimately translate into some form of meaningful action. We serve a God who is the source of all creativity, and we as believers should seek to worship God as creatively as possible.

The Good Friday service offers people an opportunity to empathise with those whose lives are characterised by pain and suffering. Turning to the scriptures, we are encouraged in the book of James to put our faith into action, because "faith without action is futile".

As a musician, I am always excited at the prospect of playing for the Good Friday services because it gives me an opportunity to minister to a wide cross-section of God's people. In my playing I attempt to capture the essence of the particular theme by the use of different tone colours. It is also quite a thrill to be given carte blanche to improvise freely as part of creating the atmosphere for worship. I look forward to accompanying the singers as well as the congregation because people do sing with much conviction. It is most humbling to be part of an experiential service that pays homage to our multi-faceted, all powerful, all loving God!

Melvin Peters

Who is my neighbour?
Ngubani umakhelwane wami?

Preacher: Fr Albert Nolan OP

Inkonzo yePhasika · Good Friday Service
Durban Exhibition Centre
Friday 21 March 2008 · 6.15am

THE NEEDS OF OUR NEIGHBOURS

In the year since the 2007 Good Friday service the need for the work of Diakonia and its member churches had been emphasised over and over again, in the continuing context of deprivation and suffering in which Diakonia was operating, as the organisation worked towards its vision of a transformed society actively working for social justice.

Against the ongoing backdrop of poverty, HIV/AIDS, crime and corruption in a country and a world where the rich get richer and the poor get poorer, Christians are called to love their neighbour as they love themselves. And so the theme for the 2008 Good Friday service on 21 March, Human Rights Day, became clear: *'Who is my neighbour?'*

WHO IS MY NEIGHBOUR?

The hall at the Durban Exhibition Centre gradually filled as the congregation quietly sang meditative chants and choruses. Some looked at the booklet in each person's place for their meditation and for taking home with them as they would take the theme back to their churches.

A large cross and two smaller crosses stood on the platform in front of the people, signifying the cross of Christ and Christ's two 'neighbours' crucified on either side.

The hall was darkened, with a spotlight on the crosses. Through the darkened hall came six hooded, anonymous figures walking slowly and hesitantly. When they got to the cross of Christ, they fell to their knees before it.

Then, one by one, they spoke out the drama of the poor and the marginalised, as they shared their stories. And the congregation responded, affirming to each of them that indeed *'You are our neighbour!'*

After a responsive prayer, one of the bible readings was Jesus' story of the Good Samaritan. Fr Albert Nolan OP preached about its meaning, linking the story to the celebration of Human Rights Day and the violations of human rights that had been committed in South Africa and were even now being committed in Zimbabwe, South Africa's neighbour. As he closed, Fr Nolan reminded the congregation that: *'My neighbour is everyone, all human beings – without exception.'*

The congregation was led in a confession of the ways in which selfishness makes people misuse God's creation, forget the cries of the needy, defy God's rule over their lives and the lives of others, and refuse to treat others as their neighbour, with dignity and love regardless of their social status, gender, nationality or religion.

Prayers of intercession were led for neighbours in poverty and sickness, those who are abused and violated, those who control government, commerce and industry, neighbours in other parts of Africa, especially in Zimbabwe and other areas undergoing mis-rule and conflict, and neighbours in places of conflict in other parts of the world, particularly in Iraq and Afghanistan, and in Palestine/Israel. Finally, a prayer was led for all present: *'That we may recognise our neighbours in time for us to take action, to make a difference for their future and for our own.'*

The congregation moved silently through the streets of Durban to the front of the City Hall, led by several groups in turn carrying the cross, and a banner challenging passers-by: *'Who is my neighbour?'*

At the City Hall the congregation joined in an affirmation that, because *'all God's people are my neighbour'*, they would work for a world where the human rights of every single person are respected. People then came forward and placed flowers on the cross, which was raised to joyful cries of *'Alleluia'*, followed by a commitment by everyone to work for a just society, in which all are recognised as neighbours.

Cardinal Wilfrid Napier OFM, Archbishop of Durban, blessed the congregation, who responded by singing the hymn which in some ways has become a symbol of the inspiration behind Diakonia's vision, mission and work, *'Who will save our land and people?'*, a hymn that has rung out since the first Good Friday service in 1985, through the struggle years, through the years of transition and is still sung in the years of transformation.

After the service the flowered cross was taken to Manning Road Methodist Church, where it stood gloriously on Easter Sunday in a sanctuary – filled floor to ceiling with beautiful flower arrangements. A testament indeed to a church community which would, in a month's time, become a home to many refugees displaced by horrendous xenophobia in the city.

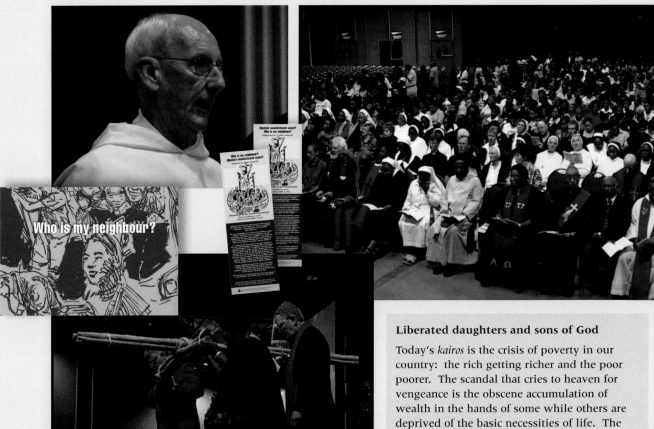

CRISIS STRIKES OUR NEIGHBOURS

Sadly, the theme *'Who is my neighbour'*, whilst highlighting a Christian duty and call to love all, served as a prophetic warning of a national tragedy, as in the weeks and months that followed the Good Friday service hundreds of foreign nationals, including women and children, lost lives or were displaced, and tens of thousands lost homes, livelihoods and belongings, and in many cases, hope.

The results of this xenophobia called for the churches to act in crisis mode. These people were neighbours – both those being attacked and the attackers. Through the involvement of Diakonia, many churches in eThekwini municipal area were inspired to reach out in a myriad of ways to those displaced, including providing food and shelter in church halls. This was a clear sign of God's welcoming hand to neighbour without exception.

Once the urgent issues were being dealt with, Diakonia joined other partners throughout the following months in ongoing discussions and briefings to look at the root causes, and to plan for a more just and peaceful way forward, including making this theme the focus of 2008's Ecumenical Conference and Diakonia's Annual Lecture.

Liberated daughters and sons of God

Today's *kairos* is the crisis of poverty in our country: the rich getting richer and the poor poorer. The scandal that cries to heaven for vengeance is the obscene accumulation of wealth in the hands of some while others are deprived of the basic necessities of life. The result of this crisis is the anger of the poor, seen in the riots demanding service delivery and the current xenophobia.

We looked with disbelief at the havoc, destruction and pain caused by our fellow South Africans on people from other countries. What has happened to our rainbow nation, our Christian faith, our *Ubuntu*?

The Oikos Journey, a theological reflection on the economic crisis in South Africa, challenged the church and society to address economic injustice, and warned us of the consequences if we did not listen to the cry of the poor. Nelson Mandela in 1994 at his inauguration was quoted as saying:

> *"Our deepest fear is not that we are inadequate. Our deepest fear is that we are powerful beyond measure. It is our light, not our darkness, that most frightens us. We are children of God. Our playing small does not serve the world: we are born to manifest the glory of God that is within us. It is in everyone. And, as we let our light shine, we consciously give other people permission to do the same. As we are liberated from our fear, our presence automatically liberates others."*

May we live as liberated daughters and sons of God.

Bishop Barry Wood OMI
*Extract from Annual Report of
the Diakonia Council of Churches 2007/2008*

Good Friday the whole year

For me the Good Friday service is not just the three hours on Good Friday: it is the whole year's event. I am saying this because, when I get involved in the planning of the service, we make dates for planning meetings and set the date immediately after one service for its evaluation. Then it goes on from there, meeting after meeting.

It is exciting when we have to choose the theme for the service. Oh my goodness, it is fascinating: everyone coming with themes. We tease them out, mix and match, until we get the theme that is acceptable to all of us. We have come up with wonderful themes, such as "Who is my neighbour?", and many other meaningful ones. I love that. The other one is when we look at the drawing of the posters and leaflets. Some of us become experts, even though we can hardly draw a circle. The other thing that always touches me is when we have to choose the preacher. This needs to involve a lot of prayer. The sermons are always inspiring.

What I am trying to say is that the Good Friday service is the outcome of a job well done.

The service has grown from Central Methodist Church to Emmanuel Cathedral to the ICC full house. It gives me satisfaction to know that this is about God receiving the praise and glory from us Christians, standing up and expressing ourselves on the streets, confessing that Jesus is the Lord, with all those multitudes, the tolling of the bells and the whole city standing still for His followers to confess Him openly.

I am very sure that God loves what He sees us do on Good Friday. I cannot imagine Good Friday in Durban without that service. I always think that we have an obligation to keep this service for almost ever, because I don't imagine what would happen to those multitudes who are dedicated to come to the service. The spirit of ecumenism overwhelms me. This is one time when nobody remembers what their denomination is.

What I want to say here is that the Good Friday service is not just about that one day. It takes the whole year.

Nelisiwe Bam
Vice Chairperson
Diakonia Council of Churches

The Raising of the Flowered Cross

God will reign
      Alleluia, alleluia.
Christ will triumph
      Alleluia, alleluia.
The Spirit moves over the world
      Alleluia, alleluia.

Commitment

In the name of Christ
      who suffered, and suffers still
         in the suffering of the world
         in the denial and deprivation of human rights,
      but who rose again
         and calls us to follow him
         into the new life of resurrection,
we commit ourselves
      to work for a society in which
         all are recognised as our neighbour
         no-one is denied their human rights
         and everyone can grow into the fullness of life
            intended by God.

Epilogue

Diakonia's first Good Friday service and procession was held in 1985, as a pilgrimage of solidarity with those unjustly held in prison.

A pilgrimage is not an escape from life. Pilgrims are on a journey with God and with a crowd of witnesses, companions, in order to immerse themselves even deeper in life. Pilgrims are preparing to continue the struggle.

Since 1987 the annual Good Friday service and procession through the streets of Durban has become a significant tradition. It has become a pilgrimage of hope as, year after year, Diakonia points in a dramatic and prophetic way to an aspect of the world's injustice to its own people.

Through a liturgy of worship, music, singing, words, drama and action, thousands of worshippers join in prayer on behalf of those who are suffering as a result of humanity's own inhumanity, ignorance or apathy. In the silent, patient walking through the streets carrying the cross, they re-enact the steps of Christ to the crucifixion, bearing the sufferings of the world as they walk.

As the crucifixion of Christ was a political act, so are the sufferings to which Diakonia draws attention year after year. Diakonia is pointing towards the root causes of suffering and

challenging worshippers to act out the abandonment of the suffering.

The Good Friday services affirm the rejection of that abandonment by those taking part. In their prayers and their pilgrimage they are saying 'NO!' to injustice, pain and despair. They are taking a public stand and preparing to take action in solidarity with those who bear the suffering.

At the climax of the pilgrimage, flowers are placed on the cross. The flowering becomes a statement of faith and hope in Christ's resurrection. Suffering becomes transformed into joy as the flowered cross is raised for all to see.

The time comes for people of God from Diakonia's member churches to make a firm commitment to continue the struggle, to work with God for the transformation of suffering into hope.

As the pilgrimage of hope comes to an end, the pilgrims leave to go their separate ways, committed to work for a world in which every person may live life in all its fullness, as God intends. And Diakonia is ready to support the pilgrims, to enable resources to be found, to facilitate the skills needed in the struggle for justice and humanity.

The Pilgrimage Continues

When hope invites us to journey
elusive, beckoning onward
but never in our grasp:
> **God of wisdom and promise
> give us courage to travel on.**

When dreams glimmer in the distance,
fading, clouded and hidden
or shining with new brightness:
> **God of wisdom and promise
> give us courage to travel on.**

When established patterns collapse
into the uncertainty of the unknown
and security dissolves into a memory:
> **God of wisdom and promise
> give us courage to travel on.**

When the illusion of success
threatens to divert us
and silence our souls' yearning:
> **God of wisdom and promise
> give us courage to travel on.**

When we think our journey has ended
in the joy of the flowered cross
only to find the end is a new beginning:
> **God of wisdom and promise
> give us courage to travel on.**

Appreciation

The names of the writers of the prayers and liturgy written for Good Friday services, as for most Diakonia publications, are seldom made public. Much has been original creative writing, from the pens (and nowadays the computers) of staff members and occasionally others. Sometimes material has been adapted from prayers or other material published by partners such as Christian Aid or CAFOD.

Similarly, analysis and historical writing is not normally acknowledged where it has been written or contracted by staff, or where it has been freely adapted by staff from sources close to Diakonia.

Those who have written and adapted for the Good Friday services, as well as those who have drawn illustrations and designed posters, have found satisfaction in the use of the ideas in the form given to them at these services, and in some cases used over and over again in private and public worship in the churches and elsewhere.

Sometimes Diakonia had to say 'no' to something offered or produced for a Good Friday service, whether this was a prayer, a drawing, a design, or even the idea for a cross. Working collectively, as Diakonia does, means reaching consensus. This is not necessarily easy to reach, especially when the art or creative writing has been more than usually 'controversial', or something that might unduly offend some members of our churches. To those whose work was 'rejected' in this way, Diakonia can only apologise – whilst deeply appreciating the spirit in which the work was conceptualised and offered to Diakonia.

We are grateful to God for the gifts of skill and talent and creativity unstintingly offered and received as these Good Friday services have been put together over the years. We know that these gifts have been offered to God in praise, humility and joy.

We are also deeply grateful to all those who participated in so many ways in leading these services, from readers to musicians, from preachers to dancers, from ushers and marshalls, to those who prepared the flowers and helped to flower the cross – and to so many others.

And, although worship of God needs no other purpose than to glorify God, we are also grateful that so many have been so moved by these Good Friday services. We are even more grateful that so many have been inspired, have discovered courage to go on with the struggle for a more just society and against injustice in God's name, and have found deep peace and joy in worshipping

together in this annual pilgrimage of hope.

To all those who have contributed in so many diverse ways, we say: God knows all your names. And your friends at Diakonia and in the churches treasure your contributions, and above all treasure you for offering yourselves unstintingly to God through Diakonia.

To those who contributed to this book we also express warm thanks. Many have shared their memories generously, people within and outside the Diakonia offices have helped to locate archival material, proof-reading has been carefully carried out. All this work is greatly appreciated.

Finally, a special thanks to Sue Britton for her skilful writing and her energy, for honing

archival material with her sharp mind, and for coordinating the various aspects of putting this book together. Her skill has contributed immensely to the existence of this invaluable resource.

Let us all look forward to many more years on this pilgrimage.

Thank you to you all.

Nomabelu Mvambo-Dandala
Executive Director,
Diakonia Council of Churches